Voices of the Tea Party

Voices of the Tea Party

By

Steve Ference

Printed in the United States of America

First Edition

Cover Design by Alvin Tostig.

Published by Lulu.com.

~July 4, 2010~

Electronic and print versions can be purchased at:

Lulu.com

Keywords: Voices of the Tea Party

Lulu.com/content/8674799

Or

Amazon.com

For Beth
And My Family

Contents

A wise and frugal government, which shall leave men free to regulate their own pursuits of industry and improvement, and shall not take from the mouth of labor the bread it has earned - this is the sum of good government.

-Thomas Jefferson

Introduction

There is a feeling that something is wrong in America. Surely, not everyone feels it, but you don't have to go far to find that just under the cheery surface, many Americans are *very* worried about the future. Even for those who pay more attention to the details of their own lives than they do to the news, there is still often the sense that *something just isn't right*.

You don't need to be politically engaged to realize why this feeling exists. Travel to small towns and cities across the country, you can see that the status quo isn't working. Take Claxton, Georgia, for example. In the center of town by the water tower that dwarfs the one or two-level buildings lining the four-way intersection, the businesses have moved out. Most of them are gone. True, Claxton is a small city of just over 2,000 people – but it's not unlike scores of other municipalities across the country. They are places that may feel about as far as you can get from Wall Street, and yet, Wall Street is often not too far from the minds of the folks who live here. Local residents may not seem quite sure where to place the blame more specifically, but no matter who deserves it, there are still all those signs sitting in the dusty shop windows that read, *For Sale,* and, *For Rent.*

They are the signs of a distraught economy, of personal economic hardship – the most visible clues that real people are really hurting. Talk with the people in town, they'll tell you that the small farmer is being pushed out of business. They're not talking about the "small farmer" in broad terms, either. They're talking about the farmer just down that road over there, the man who just can't compete anymore. Or you can talk with one business owner who will tell you that it's been a struggle to keep clients because the money has simply dried up. Even if he never really followed politics too closely, or even if he never gave much thought to that Tea Party group that he's heard something about on the news, he might say to you – in something just above a whisper - that something has to change.

More than 2,160 miles to the west, you can drive away from the neon lights that paint the desert sky each night, through the suburbs of Las Vegas. Somehow, the scene isn't that different in California or

Arizona or Florida or in your town somewhere in America. "For Sale" signs seem to be everywhere, especially in the newer developments. Although there are fewer such signs now, the impact they had on each family is still very real. Just ask anyone who's already moved to escape a personal financial mess that they may be only partially responsible for.

It's actually surprisingly easy to find someone whose life has been turned upside down in the last few years. What's hard is having a chat that just might force you to revisit your personal beliefs about how you *think* this society works. There are heart-wrenching conversations going on across the country between parents in almost every town. While their kids play in the other room, they try to manipulate the numbers in their checkbooks before they, too, will be forced to move. There are countless other stories, like those that involve lost jobs and wavering hope. As you read this, similar concerns simmer in the minds of millions of Americans who now struggle to get back to the life they had. Indeed, travel back east through the farming town of Surry, Virginia – population 260 or so – and you'll see signs nailed to the trees that straddle the space between the flat green cornfields and a thin two-lane road. These signs read, "No Incumbents," because people are looking for answers.

It is this feeling – and so much more - that has led many to start paying attention to politics, to follow the money in the wake of the Great Recession. Many folks are not only paying attention, they're also getting involved. Suddenly, in the last couple years, what we've come to know as the *Tea Party* has transformed the debate across America with rallies that have drawn hundreds of thousands of people, if not millions, who all hunger for solutions to the many problems facing the country.

They've spoken out, and they continue to speak out. And yet, while the crowds have marched in dozens of cities, even massing in Washington, DC, they will almost certainly tell you just how misunderstood they think they are. Perhaps, the misunderstanding is for good reason. Some critics haven't walked in their shoes. They haven't lived through *their* financial struggle. Add to this the fact that without a clear national platform, the Tea Party protestors often disagree among themselves on a number of issues. Complicating matters, as advocates for individual freedom, they actually seem to cherish the right to disagree with each other. They might even disagree with some of the views expressed by those interviewed for this book.

But whether they can find agreement among themselves or not, their views are often outside what has been the accepted mainstream political narrative. Many will admit that fact alone doesn't make it any easier for others to understand the movement; it creates a political dissonance with most people's current understanding of what America is all about. Many of the protestors are also unsure about where the movement might lead them or their country, if anywhere. And yet, most seem to see this moment in American history as a moment brimming with the potential to get the nation back on track.

If the Tea Party movement is the start of something, the movement itself was in many ways formed from economic frustration. Protestors abhor personal debt, so to them it follows that a growing national debt must be equally as paralyzing. That's why the Tea Partiers do agree that fiscally conservative ideals (which some detractors might call *radically* fiscally conservative ideals) are the only way to tackle the exploding debt load that somehow became taxpayers' responsibility. They worry that the next several generations of Americans will struggle to make ends meet in the *Debt Years* that they think are already upon us. They are mothers, fathers, brothers, and sisters who fear that their children will be forced to pay off all of the debt that some of the big banks racked up and then handed off to nations around the world.

However, they are concerned about more than economic issues alone. They are skeptical of both Republicans and Democrats, even though most would be more apt to vote for a candidate with an R after his or her name. Most seem to feel compelled to blame "Reid" or "Pelosi" for at least some of America's problems, whether the Congressional leaders deserve it or not. But that's just scratching the Tea Party surface. In fact, it is not a one-issue movement. You would discover that fact in just the first ten minutes of talking with anyone at a rally because you'd probably hear about debt, spending, money, entitlement programs, bailouts, taxes, inflation, healthcare, gun rights, immigration, personal liberty, over-regulation, and the size of government. They have had enough. They demand an end to the rampant corruption, condescension, and what they say is the perpetual misinterpretation of the US Constitution. Even when some do think the government has a specific role to play on an issue (such as the Gulf oil spill, for example), they might still disagree over what that exact role is. Most likely, many will also say that repeated federal and state blunders are further proof that big government is not the answer.

Out of these political concerns, the folks attending Tea Party rallies will probably tell you that they believe our current government has begun to resemble the one that the Colonists fought against more than

230 years ago. It's a statement that most of today's protestors don't make lightly. It's just another reason why it's so important to begin to understand what's on their minds. They'll argue that if the Colonists tired of working for the king's enrichment, the protestors today tire of working to see their money redistributed to people who could work but don't bother to search for a job. They'll say that if the Colonists were angered by the financial system which rewarded those who had the king's approval, then today's protestors tire of the *Corporate-Congressional Complex* where bailouts paid for by the poor and the middle-class help sustain the wealth and power of the few. If back then the Colonists felt they had little recourse to overturn laws like the one that allowed British soldiers to stay in the Colonists' homes, then today the Tea Partiers feel a similar helplessness as they worry about staying in their own homes. And speaking of homes, the protestors today don't want to pay for other people's debts while future generations get the bill for the housing crisis, a personal disaster for millions that many argue wasn't a housing crisis as much as it was a Wall Street crisis.

And so, out of the fog of financial anger, people of all different backgrounds have begun to raise their voices. They've sown together conservative and libertarian ideals out of a desire to find an answer somewhere – anywhere. True, those voices can sometimes breed controversy. Most Americans are now aware that some of the political elite have accused Tea Party supporters of being racists. Tea Party critics also say the group is anti-immigration or anti-*everything*, though most people at the rallies will tell you that if you actually attend a protest, you will find something far different. Maybe surprisingly, they will admit to you that hateful extremists protest too, but a few fringe members don't necessarily add up to a fringe group. The protestors will then spend much of their time trying to explain to you how the racial issue misses the point anyway, that most of the people releasing some steam at the protests really do seem to be common people with uncommon concerns about their country.

That's where this book comes in. This project is simply the result of attending a number of rallies as a local reporter and then going home to find that so much of the national coverage never seemed to match up with what I saw and heard. The topics I found the TV pundits talking about after I had just attended a local Tea Party protest seemed to only vaguely resemble the conversations that I had only hours before. That's why sometimes, even if there is plenty of room for disagreement on specific political topics, a reporter has to write something he never set out to write simply because no one else seems to be writing it. In other words, if a million people march in Washington, DC, to demand serious - even drastic - changes to the way things are done, it should be up to *someone* to share a few of their stories and explain why they show up at such rallies.

Whether the Tea Partiers are correct in their beliefs or not is another matter altogether. However, when individuals speak of the coming "Second American Revolution," or they say that it's already upon us, it seems it would be wise to understand what drives those people to protest. It's especially true in an age where ideas are shared at the speed of thought, an age where a *Viral Revolution* can awaken Americans to new ideas before the pundits and politicians who shape mainstream thought even become aware of it. No, the protestors' thoughts are not shared here in this book for the truth of the matter, but, rather, to understand their viewpoint and how they may continue to shape our understanding of America.

During the last year or so, I've had to make sense of everything from conspiracy theories to the United States financial system, learning so much about a new way of seeing the world that I previously knew little about. The bottom line: though you may disagree with many of the ideas shared by those who agreed to be interviewed for this book, there is little chance you'll forget what they say anytime soon.

I could have interviewed hundreds of people, but the truth is, there are common threads tying most of the Tea Party attendees together. The goal of this book is not to cover every argument made at the rallies, nor is it to dive into a dense discussion of how the movement is impacting present-day America. Instead, the goal of this book is to share the stories of a handful of Americans who are raising their voices as they search for solutions. They are the voices you might hear if you struck up a conversation at any Tea Party. They are the people you would meet if you walked up to a group of protesters and introduced yourself as a reporter who is writing a book on what people at these rallies believe. For this project the conversations often began with the question, "Why are you here?" I could never have predicted how deeply we would go down the political rabbit hole. If I heard something surprising, I asked them why they believe what they do. It was never a debate, but a discussion where my aim was to understand just a little more about them personally and how they see the United States of America today and tomorrow, without lofty political chatter or complicated theories.

Each interviewee's story is written with an attempt to capture the feel of the conversation. The book has been kept as brief as possible to allow even the busiest reader a seat at the Tea Party table, a place where you can evaluate the ideas for yourself. Figuring out how valid their point of view really is may actually get easier as time passes, too. A few of those interviewed made predictions that can be used to judge their ideas. Either way, they offer perspective that can help provide answers to a number of questions being asked around the country, such as: What does the Tea Party really stand for? Why are they so angry? Will their anger last? Who will become the movement's leader? Will there ever be a national leader? Will the Tea Party turn violent or stay peaceful? Do they all believe in conspiracy theories? Are Tea Parties really a gathering of racists? If they're not racists, are they people who hate immigrants? And what would the United States of America look like if, for instance, the people of the Tea Party got what they wanted?

These are questions that are answered quite differently, depending on who you ask. But few have been asking without an agenda, so it's time to have an honest conversation. It's time to give up the thought that ignoring or even denigrating the protestors will just make them all go away. Usually, the best disinfectant for bad ideas is sunlight, an open-minded look at what's really being said and done. That way, everyone can see just how valuable – or valueless – this Tea Party movement really is. Or just maybe, the folks carrying their bright yellow flags actually do have a good idea or two that can improve America.

No matter what your political beliefs are, as more Americans look at their country's vital signs and then search for answers to the problems facing us all, there is a certain value to hearing what they have to say. Hopefully this book adds just a little more context to the Tea Party movement as it gives the Tea Party protestors a chance to talk about what motivates them most, in their own voices.

-Steve Ference

Smithfield, Virginia

"I sincerely believe... that banking establishments are more dangerous than standing armies, and that the principle of spending money to be paid by posterity under the name of funding is but swindling futurity on a large scale."

--Thomas Jefferson to John Taylor, 1816.

Chapter I

The Gold-Star Mom

"Glory is something that some men chase and others find themselves stumbling upon, not expecting it to find them. Either way it is a noble gesture that one finds bestowed upon them. My question is when does glory fade away and become a wrongful crusade, or an unjustified means by which consumes one completely?"

-Marc Alan Lee's Letter Home

When you first meet Debbie Lee, it's impossible to miss the warmth flowing from her every word. Her eyes sparkle like those of the proudest mother. But her eyes have seen far more than a mother should ever have to endure. When you do speak with her, she'll probably tell you about Marc, her youngest son. "He was amazing," she says, her voice trying to convey just how much he means to her.

She says she tried to give Marc all she could as a single-mother, home-schooling him when she was able. But it wasn't easy. She had been through so much. "I married at a very young age to my children's father who was an alcoholic and a drug abuser, so it was a very difficult four-and-a-half years," Lee says. "And he tried to kill me twice. At that point, when I started watching some of the aggression possibly transfer to my children, I woke up and I divorced the man." Time passed, but she would face other hurdles; her second husband dealt with a number of personal demons himself, and he took his own life. So she focused on her children. She taught them about life and God and persevering because like all children, hers too would have to fight their own battles.

Still, Marc always seemed able to rise above the daily challenges, often doing it with humor. "I schooled him a little bit at a Christian school, and he got 'class clown' two years in a row," she says. "And I'm like, 'Oh great. How's this going to get you to college? What's this going to do?' He had an amazing sense of humor - that no matter what you were going through or what was going on - he could get you to laugh and raise your spirits.

"He always was just kind of pushing the envelope," laughs Lee. She looks down and draws on the desk with her finger, remembering past times. The pride she feels for her son is palpable with every word she speaks. "He started playing soccer his freshman year in high school. He never played soccer before. Stunk at it. He was a terrible soccer player, but with perseverance and determination, I would see him hour after hour, day after day, kicking the ball, juggling the ball, bouncing the ball one-hundred times on his head until it dropped. He ended up being an amazing soccer player. He was the youngest junior varsity soccer coach we ever had at his high school. He tried out for the professional team in Colorado, but the night before tryouts he blew his knee out, had to come out (of the tryouts). But he wouldn't give up. When he saw a goal worth fighting for he would work for it."

"I have seen war. I have seen death, the sorrow that encompasses your entire being as a man breathes his last. I can only pray and hope that none of you will ever have to experience some of these things I have seen and felt here."

Perhaps Marc didn't originally set out on the path he followed, but he decided he wanted to become a Navy Seal. It was a tempting path that his mind often revisited even as he attended college. He studied the bible and theology but then switched to law. Still, he couldn't escape the desire to see if he could succeed in the military. "He actually went through three different BUD/S (Basic Underwater Demolition/SEAL) classes," says Lee. He began in class number 238, but during *hell week*, which many people consider to be the most strenuous and challenging military training in the world, "He got water inside his lungs and outside his lungs, and they had done a medical check on him and said, *we got to yank you.*" To come through such rigorous training only to miss the cut because of a physical complication devastated her son. His mind still hungered to achieve his goal, but the higher-ups decided they couldn't risk it. "He said, 'No, no, I can do this. I'm good I can do this,'" Lee says, putting herself in her son's place. "He was a couple hours short of being rolled forward with the class, so instead he was rolled backwards. He had to start all over again with class 239."

Marc wouldn't graduate with class 239, either. "Maya, his wife, they fell in love," Lee explains. "And she convinced him he didn't want to be a Navy SEAL. So he got to *hell week* a second time and dropped on request and was assigned to the USS Enterprise." But Marc was torn once again. As he served on the Enterprise, he lacked a sense of fulfillment. "I remember him calling one night saying, 'Hey, Mom. What am I supposed to do? Maya doesn't want me to do this. I really want to do this.'" His mother, who finds comfort by trusting in God, asked her son, "Are you sure that's what God wants you to do?" He told her it was. "And I said, 'If you're not doing what God wanted you to do, you're going to come home and yell at your wife and kick the dog, scream at the kids, and nobody's going to be happy. You need to do whatever it takes and jump through whatever hoops and get your butt back there." He did jump through hoops, refocusing all of his effort. "It took him a year," she says. He finally earned one more chance to become a SEAL.

Though Marc fought hard just for the opportunity to succeed, Lee says her son also fought hard for others. His fellow SEALS told her about one training scenario that lasted an entire week. A whole *week* simulating being dropped off or lost in the middle of a war zone as the SEALS try to avoid being captured. It meant a week with no food, or at least, it meant a week of eating whatever food they could find. "They're hunted, they're out hiding in the jungle or the forest," Lee explains. "They had hid some food, so as they went throughout the week, they could find a little food. And they went back on Thursday to find their food, and it wasn't there," she says. "They don't know if animals got there or the instructors found it. Marc had hid his in a little better place, or deeper or something, and his was there. He opened it and gave it all away. He didn't take a bite." She pauses for a moment, almost like she's remembering what she would have witnessed had she been there to see the whole scenario unfold. "He was not the perfect kid by any means. None of my children were. I wasn't the perfect mom, so how could I have perfect kids?" But perfect or not, he had graduated second in his class, class number 251. Marc was a Navy SEAL.

"I have felt fear and have felt adrenaline pump through my veins making me seem invincible. I will be honest and say that some of the things I have seen here are unjustified and uncalled for. However, for the most part we are helping this country. It will take more years than most expect, but we will get Iraq to stand on its own feet."

Marc was deployed to Iraq in 2006 - Ramadi, Iraq - to be exact. Even if most Americans can't exactly point to it on a map, it's a city that has been in the news far too often during the war for the numerous battles between US-led forces and the local insurgents. Marc experienced some of those battles.

Marc's fellow SEALS would later tell his mother that they had spent hours planning the battle that was to take place on August 2nd. "I'm sure knowing the battle they were going in, the tension was there," she says. "And Marc, with his antics, kept them laughing and their spirits up. That's just who he was. He was a young man. He valued other people's lives more than his own which is extremely unusual to find in today's society. We have been taught, *take care of yourself, you can't take care of everybody else. Me first.* I read story after story after story about Marc – things he had done for other people that were selfless, not just standing up in the direct line of fire to defend his buddies."

Following their battle plans, the SEALS set up on a rooftop as the sun scorched any skin that wasn't covered by their protective gear or heavy backpacks. Soon, Marc and the team traded gunfire with insurgents who were hiding inside another building. In the 115-degree heat, one of his brothers-in-battle was seriously injured when a bullet ripped through his body. Lee says that's when Marc protected his team. He could have stayed down. He could have hunched behind the rooftop barrier. But he knew he had to cover his fellow SEALS if they were to evacuate his wounded comrade from the rooftop. He stood up to draw the insurgents' attention, ducking back down as bullets tore through the air, missing him. He stood again, drawing more fire while his team moved their injured fellow SEAL to safety.

After the exchange of bullets had calmed, the SEALS thought they had figured out where the insurgents were hiding. They decided to go after them. The enemy, after all, would continue firing at them or any American soldiers who came here in the future. That's when they began clearing houses, floor by floor, room by room.

"Most of what I have seen here I will never really mention or speak of, only due to the nature of those involved. I have seen a man give his food to a hungry child and family. Today I saw a hospital that most of us would refuse to receive treatment from. The filth and smell would allow most of us to not be able to stand to enter, let alone get medicine from. However, you will be relieved to know that coalition forces have started to provide security for and supply medicine and equipment to help aid in the cause."

Halfway across the world, in Arizona, Lee was celebrating her birthday with friends. Her actual birthday had been a week before, but it was a time to at least *try* to let loose with the small group that had supported her throughout her son's deployment. Lee explains how on that night, "One of my friends had given me one of the Willow Tree statues, named *Courage*." Her friend told her it was the perfect gift because with all she had been through, *courage* seemed the perfect word to describe how Lee got through her son's deployment. The women shared a few tears and a few of their worries, but they also shared each other's strength. "We had no clue in the next half-hour how much courage I was going to need to get through life," Lee says.

"As I was driving home that night, I knew when Marc was here - and he was here in March just before he deployed - I knew when he left, he wasn't coming back home. I'm not a worrier, I'm not a fretter," Lee says. "But something inside - I'm not sure if it was God trying to prepare me, *he won't be back home*." Lee starts to choke up as she remembers.

On that night in 2006, Lee was almost home. As she drove, she received a phone call from her oldest son. "Hey, mom," he said. There was no emotion in his voice. "Where are you? How long will it take you to come home?" he asked.

"I don't know, five, seven minutes. Why?" Lee asked, listening for any clue that there was nothing seriously wrong.

"You just need to come home."

"His voice didn't share any heartbreak or fear," Lee says. "It was just matter of fact. And as I drove home that night, there was a Psalm from my past that says, *I put my hope in you O Lord. Trust in you, I will not be shaken, knowing that you will see me through, I put my hope in you.* And I just said that over and over and over and over the entire time. And I got to the intersection, the main intersection where we live. And I saw probably five fire trucks and three police cars and emergency vehicles." She was actually relieved. "My thought was - it's just my house. My house blew up, that's all that's wrong." She never did find out why all the emergency vehicles had stopped near her home.

She parked her car. "My son was just pacing on the sidewalk," Lee says, her voice cracking as she remembers that awful blur of a night. She opened her car door and stepped out. Her son, who had just told her to get home, looked at his mother and said, "Mom, the Navy is here."

"And you know," Lee says, stopping for a second, trying to hold her emotions in, "you know when you have someone serving and the military shows up at your house, it's not good because they'll call if there's been injury." She fell on her son's shoulders and started crying.

A Navy Chaplain, an officer, and another man in uniform helped her inside. They comforted her as they glanced at the home they had found themselves in this time, on this night. "We can tell by looking at your home that you're a woman of faith," one of the men said. "And you're going to need to rely on God to get through what we need to tell you."

Lee breaks down while she remembers: "They told me that my son, Marc Alan Lee, had been killed in action."

She says the hurt cannot be translated or spoken into words, but Lee puts it simply: "You get news like that, it forever changes your life. And my small group came in shortly after that and stayed with me, cried with me, prayed with me, cried some more, prayed some more." They stayed with her until about one-thirty in the morning.

Exhausted and emotionally drained, Lee tried to get some rest. "And I knew in the quiet of the night, I couldn't sleep," she says. "I knew where my strength came from, and I picked up my Bible and turned to Psalm 27. It starts out, 'The Lord is my light and my salvation whom shall I fear'...And Marc was a believer, and I knew that God was telling me that Marc wasn't afraid at the end. Marc died instantly. There wasn't lots of pain or suffering. And in the midst of that battle, he was - that was his desire to dwell in the house of the Lord all the days of his life, and he was there now. And the rest of the verse and the chapter just gave me comfort.

"I read that Psalm at the service, and I had such strength that God gave me and such confidence in Him - it even surprised me the strength He gave me. And people came up to me after and said they were so inspired and so encouraged by his mother getting up there. And if *you* could get through this, we knew *we* could," Lee says. She was only doing the best she could. Truthfully, it wasn't just an impossible day for her, but a harsh realization for the other Navy families too. "For you could see in the eyes of these wives and mothers, it was like, *oh my gosh, we could lose a loved one. But if Debbie can get through this, we can have that same hope and strength that we can get through it*," she says.

Somehow, Lee managed to find her voice as she comforted others. "When I talked to Marc's teammates when they would call...I was so concerned for them, how they would go back into battle, dealing with the grief and the loss of Marc," Lee says. "So I would try to give them hope and encouragement. I ended up having an amazing relationship - I had five of the SEAL's in the home the week Marc died. Marc always tried to explain the brotherhood thing, but I said, *I'm sure you get close to these guys*, but first of all, I didn't believe them. *They can't be your brothers, and you didn't grow up with them your whole life. How could it possibly be as close as you are with your brothers?* But when they were in my home, I saw how much they loved Marc, how deeply they grieved. The light went on – *oh my gosh, these really are his brothers."* She also realized that, "if those are his brothers, then I've adopted and inherited a whole bunch of boys. To this day they're still in my life…babies are born and I get pictures on my cell phone. I get invited to their weddings. I'm a very blessed woman."

At that time in her life, she had no idea where the loss of her son would lead her. "But from that point, basically, as I said, I would walk through whatever doors God opened," Lee says. Soon, those doors would open wider than she could have possibly imagined. "I've been with President Bush six times, I've been up on stage with Tim McGraw at the Academy Country Music Awards. I couldn't even begin to tell you – I've been to the Vice President's house for a Christmas party. General Petraeus responds to me within 20 minutes when I send him an e-mail." He is the man who President Obama would later choose to take over command of the Afghanistan war. She pauses, almost as if she's surprised at the thought. "I'm just Marc's mom. I wasn't anyone famous or special, but God gave me a mission to stand up for the troops and for their families."

As she continued to support the troops, Lee found a path leading her to Tea Parties around the country. "That's where it kind of started for me," she says. "I followed *Move America Forward* with a cross-country tour to support our troops, and I decided I could go along and honor our troops and thank them and wave the flag and follow behind. The first stop that we were at, they asked if I could share Marc's story. I shared from my heart, and since then, I spoke at every one of their rallies and tours and events. I've done seven cross-country tours, I've been to Iraq and Guantanamo because I'm very passionate."

Lee says she didn't agree with all of President Bush's policies, but she will never forget the first time she met him. "What a man of noble character. A genuine, humble man – and sincere." She had written the president a letter after her Congressman heard her story and urged her to share it. "Even though I lost my son," she says, "I still believed (the war) was the right thing to do…I started to write on one of Marc's old writing pads that I found in the house where we used to live, and I just thought back to 9/11 and when I found out. My oldest son was in the Marines. My son-in-law was in the Army. Marc was in the Navy. And I could see the handwriting on the wall. I knew this was going to be a personal war. I didn't understand how personal it would be." As she searched for the words to write down for the president, Lee says that on "that very night, President Bush sat down and wrote me a letter - an amazing letter - and said he would be honored to meet me. In October, he was here in Arizona," she says, excited to share the details of her visit. "So they called and made arrangements. When I met him, there was no photographer there. There was no media. There was just my son and his wife, myself, and the President. No Secret Service - nobody else was in the room. And when he walked in, tears in his eyes, you could tell he cared about me and Marc's death."

President Bush pulled a chair next to her, she says, recounting the meeting. *This is where I want to sit, right next to the hero's mother*, she remembers him saying. *You're going to need your faith to get you through this*, the president told her. The four sat and talked together for a full 35 minutes.

But once President Bush left office after his second term, she says the new administration treated her differently. According to Lee, meetings with President Obama kept getting postponed. It could be argued that the President had to contend with an economy on the brink of collapse, among other important issues consuming his time. But it was Lee's *perception* of the new tone in Washington that still bothers her. After several postponements, "I got a letter from him that is probably a form letter that's sent to all Gold-Star families," Lee says. "It didn't mention Marc by name, didn't address any of the things I wanted to talk with him about. Kind of a trite, *so sorry for your loss*. You could see the contrast between the two men who led our nation. It was stamped on the bottom, it wasn't even signed. And in June they said they'd postpone it until the end of the year, and I never heard anything.

"I am not a racist," she says. "It has nothing to do with the color of their skin. Bush could have been black and Obama could be white, and my feelings would still be the same because of their character, the choices they've made. Our troops - today - are going to be giving up their lives for you and for me and for the freedoms that we have in America," Lee says. "So when we started to see this political change and the things that our men and women are fighting for, I knew I had to speak up about that too. And to tell people, don't waste the sacrifice of what our men and women have given, what they have fought for." Lee speaks almost as if she's pleading with me. "I feel like our country is turning the corner in the wrong direction. I know in my own home, if I don't have the money to buy something, I don't buy it. It's common sense, and we've gotten so far in debt. Our grandchildren and great-grandchildren aren't even going to be able to pay off the interest on the debt. So it's just like because of our troops and their sacrifice - what they're still fighting for - that I need to stand and fight over here so when they do come home, we do still have the same freedoms they have fought and bled and died for."

So now, *she* fights. "After doing the Tea Party Express tour and stopping in almost 60 cities and watching crowds, probably the average-sized crowd was a couple thousand people," Lee says. "And we would ask, *how many of you haven't been to a Tea Party event before? How many of you haven't been to a political rally before?* And it was always the majority that were there. And to me, that encourages my heart, saying, *OK, people are finally getting up out of their La-Z-Boys. They're not yelling at their TV's anymore.* They're not screaming around their homes anymore, saying, *this isn't right.* They're saying, *OK, it's time for me to do something. I have to get up.* And they're getting educated. They're coming together and finding they're not alone.

"I think there's a huge tidal wave that's heading to DC in November. And I think they haven't a clue as to how many people are upset, how many will use not only their voice, but their vote to make a difference. To me, that's encouraging. I think we're going to see some major changes. I think it started when we got Scott Brown, who they said there was no chance for who won that race." Brown had seemingly come from behind to beat Democratic candidate Martha Coakley for a Congressional seat in Massachusetts. While some blamed the loss on missteps during her campaign, others felt the Tea Party provided Brown the tailwind needed for him to win the election. "We're seeing Sharron Angle in Nevada against Harry Reid, and I think the last I saw she was up over him."

At the five dozen Tea Party rallies that she has attended, Lee says she saw a diverse mass of people tied together not by political party, but by their common belief system. "There's so many around the country saying, *we need to take our roots back,*" she says. "The conservatives are standing up. It doesn't have anything to do with Democrat, Republican, or Independent. This has to do with the principles that our country was founded on. It has to do with the Constitution our country was founded on. I can't tell you how many people I know (who) have read the

Constitution recently who never read it in their life. It's like, oh goodness, you know? It's sad they haven't...been educated, but it's encouraging that they're finally saying, *I want to get educated, I want to read the documents of our Founding Fathers. I want to understand the country that we're founded upon.* So to me, I think there's hope and encouragement, though."

That's why, when she turns on her television to catch the national news, she says she doesn't understand some of the reports on the Tea Party rallies. "That's what was so repulsive to me. On the tour we were seeing crowds that were not angry mobs," she says. "They may be angry and upset with the way our country's headed, but they're not out there being angry and attacking people and screaming and yelling and throwing out racist remarks. We had a mix of people...my children are half Spanish. So to say we're a racist, angry mob, you know, we saw almost the opposite. For those of us who are white, we almost didn't get any media attention. They didn't want to talk to us, you know? We almost saw the reverse discrimination." She chalks it up to "liberal media bias." She says when she visited a combat zone in Iraq – the first Gold-Star Mother to visit the area where her son had died - no mainstream media outlet covered it. She says it seemed to her at the time like no one wanted to report on the progress she saw in Iraq, either. "It's not just about Marc, it's all about those men and women. Whether it was World War I or World War II, Vietnam or Korea, all of those, those are true heroes who have fought, bled, and died for the Constitution and the freedoms we have - and for me. I'm passionate about this, that because of their sacrifices, I've got to stand for my country. I've got to alert people, challenge them, encourage them, use my belief to bring them together to save this country."

It's why she chose to travel with the Tea Party Express as the group toured the country – another chance to share her voice. "I've always been politically active and have taken a strong stance on moral issues, on abortion, on homosexuality, on some of those moral issues as a believer," she says, "because I'm committed to what God's word says. For our troops, when I started speaking out for them, I was very active and on Capitol Hill a lot. I know a lot of Congressman and Senators personally, just from making sure they get the equipment they need, that they're paid, that the VA takes care of them."

Whenever she thinks justice is being denied, it ignites an internal fire, sparking her to urge others to do what's right. "I don't see that being done in our country," she says. "I see a lack of respect for life, for the beginning of life, or the end of life. I see disregard for –

economically – how they're spending our money - what they're spending it on, the choices they're making. I think they're trying, that the government has gotten way too big and trying to legislate things that, although (they) might be wise things to do, should still be my choice as an American whether to do those things or not do those things. We're seeing…out-of-control spending in our government that has gotten so far from what our Founding Fathers meant for this to be."

But it isn't only the support for the troops, nor is it the economy that brings her to the Tea Party rallies. It's also the arrogance she perceives from America's leaders, "trying to act as though Americans are too stupid to know what's right for us," she says. "So they have to step in and legislate and do what they think is good. And that's repulsive for me to see that kind of attitude." She says healthcare is an issue that has focused her anger: "I think the healthcare reform (was) the lack of regard to listen to us American people." Lee says she heard that some in Congress actually ignored the people's outcry against the bill. "There were phones that were taken off the hook so when people called in, they didn't have to talk to them." True or not, various news reports indicate a large call volume around the time the healthcare legislation was voted on. Some believe the calls clogged the phone system, while others, like Lee, aren't so sure. Either way, it probably helps to make her point. "You've seen numbers from 60 to 86% of people who did not support the healthcare reform the way that it was put together and the way that they keep adding all these other attachments," she says. "Just the size of the bill alone should say something."

Then, Lee proceeds to mention something that so many in the Tea Party have mentioned before - a name that keeps coming up. "Nancy Pelosi said, *Oh we need to pass this bill so we know what's in it*," Lee paraphrases. Speaker Pelosi had said almost those exact words in March of 2010 at the 2010 Legislative Conference for the National Association of Counties. To be exact, Pelosi had said: "But we have to pass the bill so that you can find out what is in it, away from the fog of the controversy." It had sent conservatives ballistic. "Well, that's like me saying, *I'm going to write a check and later I'll figure out if there's money in my account to cover it or not*," says Lee. "There are absurd things happening in our government – leaders, who, it appears to me, the power has gone to their head. And the abuse of power is unreal."

It's why Debbie Lee urges those who identify with the Tea Party to stand up. "I want to tell them to use their voices, use their vote," she says passionately. "I think we have been so fearful or intimidated, afraid you're going to offend your neighbor if you talk about politics. You know the old adage is the two things you don't talk about (are) politics and religion. I think that's why our country has gotten to the place it has. We need to think out loud. We need to be vocal. We need to share what we know. People have gained the majority of what they know from the nightly news. It is so slanted. They've got wrong information. A perfect example is what's going on right now in Arizona with the immigration (law) that our Governor just signed." Numerous protests had been held across the country by those who disagreed with the law, claiming it would lead to citizens losing their civil rights by being questioned for looking like a minority. But Lee disagrees. "I'm so proud of (Governor Jan Brewer). And yet it's getting so twisted to say we're going to do all this stuff that's not even in the bill. If it wasn't such a serious issue, it would be humorous."

She urges people to read the original documents – the Constitution, the Declaration of Independence. "We need to be fighting here at home. And I'm not talking about picking up weapons or arms and battling that way. We need to be fighting with our *voices* and our *votes*. We need to inform when our neighbors around us maybe don't have the right information. We need to challenge them - *here's what I found when I did my research, these are the things*. We need to be coming together at events and organizing, so we can make a difference. American people are taking this country back one step at a time," she says. "I'm encouraged to know so many patriots are willing to come along, so I don't have to do this alone."

Often, she does feel alone without her son. The date of Marc's death, August 2nd, seems to come and go, and Lee says it doesn't get easier. "I got several quilts from a few people when Marc first died, but other than that, I haven't had anybody that sends me a card on the anniversary of Marc's death, saying our country remembers. No one remembers him on his birthday - it's a difficult day - or Mother's Day…that's a tough day when you've lost a child."

Feeling at times like she's adrift at sea after the loss of her Navy SEAL – the first SEAL killed in the Iraq War – she honors her son and the others who have died as best she can. "I purchased a home in October of last year, so families of the fallen can come stay for free," she says. "It has guestrooms and a swimming pool and hot tub, so it feels a little more like a resort. It's called the *Heroes' Hope Home*. That's what it's for - to honor their heroes, to remember them. There will be a large-screen monitor that will flash the pictures of the fallen. Just a place where they can come get some hope…Just a place where they know they're not alone, that the sacrifice of their loved one isn't forgotten. They can be honored and taken care of."

It's a big project that was even the subject of a local news report in her Arizona hometown. She's been doing so much work to get the home ready, but she believes it's the little things she does for those in the military that matter the most. "I have a card that I hand out that says, *thank you for serving*," she says. "If they're standing in line to pay for their meal, I'll go up to pay for their meal or coffee or milkshake. Something little…you can always take a situation, a bad situation - a hard situation - and try to find the positive in it somewhere. I was determined to do that in life. I didn't have a choice the day Marc died. But I did have a choice the way that I handled that and what I did with that. I could have a pity party or turn to drugs or alcohol to kill the pain because it is - it's the deepest pain I've ever known. Or I could take that and make something good out of it and continue to honor Marc and continue to honor the men and women and thank them and make sure that they're loved and taken care of - and continue to fight for this country - so it does remain the country that our Founding Fathers intended for it to be."

It's exactly what Marc wrote about in his last letter home, before that August battle in Iraq when he risked his own future by deciding to stand up:

"I try to do my part over here, but the truth is over there, United States, I do nothing but take. Ask yourself when was the last time you donated clothes that you hadn't worn out. When was the last time you paid for a random stranger's cup of coffee, meal or maybe even a tank of gas? When was the last time you helped a person with the groceries into or out of their car?

Think to yourself and wonder what it would feel like if when the bill for the meal came and you were told it was already paid for. More random acts of kindness like this would change our country and our reputation as a country. It is not unknown to most of us that the rest of the world looks at us with doubt towards our humanity and morals.

I am not here to preach or to say look at me, because I am just as at fault as the next person. I find that being here makes me realize the great country we have and the obligation we have to keep it that way.

The 4th has just come and gone and I received many emails thanking me for helping keep America great and free. I take no credit for the career path I have chosen;

I can only give it to those of you who are reading this, because each one of you has contributed to me and who I am.

However what I do over here is only a small percent of what keeps our country great. I think the truth to our greatness is each other. Purity, morals and kindness, passed down to each generation through example. So to all my family and friends, do me a favor and pass on the kindness, the love, the precious gift of human life to each other so that when your children come into contact with a great conflict that we are now faced with here in Iraq, that they are people of humanity, of pure motives, of compassion.

This is our real part to keep America free! HAPPY 4th Love Ya

Marc Lee

P.S. Half way through the deployment can't wait to see all of your faces

Chapter II

The Attorney

"Well, we don't know how many people are there (at the Searchlight, Nevada Tea Party protest), but how many ever people we have, I'm glad they're there...I hope they have a good occasion. That's what America is all about. It's a democracy, and people have a voice and they should use it."

-Senate Majority Leader Harry Reid

KTNV.com News Report

March 27, 2010

Youtube.com, posted by speakmymind02

Jim Ostrowski attends Tea Parties, but for him it's really only the logical extension of what he's been doing for years. He helps organize local campaigns for candidates who believe in small government, and he writes books on the little things each American can do to return the country to its roots. Just before he gave the interview for this book, he played his role in yet another way - using his legal background to argue for a fundamental change to the ways that the government spends taxpayers' money.

Ostrowski calls it "The Pork Lawsuit." Though you may not have heard of it, the case is an attempt to stop government from funneling tax money to private businesses in the name of economic development. In the press release he sent out to the various media outlets that mostly ignored it, he summed up the case as "an effort by fifty New York citizens to end billions of dollars of illegal corporate welfare." He named top state leaders in the court documents, although, the case had already been shot down by a lower court. However, on this day, he was given another chance, a small sliver of hope from the possibility that an appeal might be granted. He had ten minutes to convince a panel of five justices to see things his way.

If you've never attended appellate court oral arguments, you'd probably be surprised at the intensity of the proceedings. Ostrowski stands at the lectern, his voice amplified by a microphone. Five justices sit in their thickly padded leather chairs twenty feet in front of him, elevated slightly. The large marble wall and richly finished wood give the courtroom a powerful presence even without the strong gazes of the justices.

Ostrowski begins with a brief explanation of the history behind the case as he sees it. His hands grab the lectern as he speaks; if he's nervous, they don't waver an inch to show it. He talks about how his state has been banned from directly giving tax money to businesses since the 1800's. In the 1950's a number of politicians wanted to change that, but the Constitutional Convention around that time failed to allow it. Ostrowski says that's when a number of state agencies came into existence; if the state couldn't *directly* give money to corporations, the politicians surmised they could get around the problem. Their plan, he says, was to funnel tax money to agencies which would then distribute the cash to companies as they saw fit.

Not a minute into his argument, the justices pounce. Taking turns, they fire several rounds of probing questions. Ostrowski responds by saying that it boils down to the simple point that the politicians can't "evade" the Constitution. "They say they can do indirectly what they cannot do directly." The justices ponder the idea.

Almost as soon as he starts, Ostrowski's time ends. An attorney for the state takes his place, fanning out his papers. He tries to look at the justices as much as he can, but mostly, he looks at his papers. The justices pepper him with questions as he explains how the agencies are tasked with creating jobs. A couple minutes later, another attorney takes over the argument on behalf of one of the companies that allegedly benefits from the state "grants" in question. She speaks for five minutes, also taking question after question. Her words flow quickly and intensely. She seems to argue that contracts exist between corporations and the state agencies, so striking down the current system could cause major economic harm. In less than a half-hour the blur of words is over. Attorneys for another case stand and prepare for the next onslaught of questioning.

In a nearby building a short time later, Ostrowski is left to wonder what will become of the case – a legal argument that seems to have plenty of connections to the ideology shared by many in the Tea Party. "It's been building for a long time," he says, "and people are finally getting the feeling that something has to be done now, or it's going to be too late." He speaks with few pauses and no superfluous words to fill his sentences. "Lots of people who normally are not involved are getting involved, and I think that says a lot. People don't normally get involved in politics. They're very concerned about what's going on in the country."

The 52-year-old says he didn't start out with such a libertarian view. "I was a liberal democrat, although anti-war, pro-civil liberties, and skeptical about the Drug War. So I, over the years, moved to being more of the libertarian," he says. "I've never been a conservative. Which puts me somewhat at odds with some of the people in the movement. I'm basically a hard-core libertarian."

These details might sound too political, perhaps too *inside-baseball* for some folks, but it's a point of contention within some Tea Party circles. Most Americans seem to speak about the Tea Party as a *conservative* movement. Here, Ostrowski argues that *conservative* isn't the best word to describe it. "There's a big difference," he explains. "The conservatives loved George Bush. And the libertarians strongly disliked George Bush. In civil liberties he's bad, in Asian land wars – we're not into that. Certainly he wasn't a fiscal conservative. I started attacking Bush on his budget policies on April of 2001. So when people say, *where were you when there was the Bush administration*, they don't understand that about one-third of the movement is libertarian. We were bashing Bush consistently, particularly my version of libertarianism which is based on and associated with the Mises Institute and LewRockwell.com. It's a very anti-Washington version of libertarianism."

He sums up the internal Tea Party battle as a question about who would be its best leader. On the one side, there's Ron Paul, the Texas Congressman and recent presidential candidate (his son had recently made headlines running for Congress in Kentucky). On the other side, there's Sarah Palin, the former Alaska Governor who ran as John McCain's Vice Presidential hopeful. More recently, she has toured the country giving speeches and appearing on Fox News. "The movement is split into those two different camps," Ostrowski says. "They agree on a lot of things. But there is that underlying tension which hasn't been a problem so far, but it will in 2012 because we're going to be looking for a Ron Paul or a Ron Paul-type candidate, and they're going to be looking for a Sarah Palin-type candidate. And the two will often not support the same candidate."

Although the Tea Party activists might strain to choose a certain leader, Ostrowski says the real story is simply that more and more people are showing up at rallies and looking for answers. "I've been a libertarian for decades," he says. He talks about how some of his friends and family members whom he has debated for years seem to have come around - or at least softened their resistance to Ostrowski's ideas. However, it took some time. "There have been a lot of arguments, but I think we've come to a truce," he laughs. "But I think people are beginning to see, *you know, Jim, I think you were on to something all those years.* The country is moving in my direction. I haven't changed. The country is moving in my direction on so many issues. There's people calling me who didn't used to call me. There's people who want meetings with me that didn't used to. I used to be Don Qixote, and now I'm a player." He explains that he has no interest in government power or running for office. But with hundreds of thousands – if not millions - in the country swinging towards his political perspective, he believes that with his writings and his legal work that he is making a difference. "I am now somebody who has a real world impact in what's going on."

Like so many others involved with the movement, Ostrowski is most concerned with the economy. He reiterates his point that his anger isn't the result of any one administration. In fact, some of the people who enjoy talking about some rather dense political theory will argue that the movement is very much a reaction to the New Deal policies of President Roosevelt. The argument goes, if back then Americans asked for government to protect them in the midst of the Great Depression, a growing number of Americans had come full circle during this economic crisis, seeing such big-government policies as part of the problem. "The bank bailout," Ostrowski says, shaking his head. "*This* started with the bank bailouts and the bailouts to GM. And this happened under the Bush administration. So again, the media is distorting the history because they apparently don't remember it or want to distort it. Now there's also an issue of subsidies (for) people who made bad mortgage decisions. But those people were often not living in the home. Some were just speculators, not that there is anything wrong with speculation per se, and many of them were these people who bought these McMansions that they couldn't afford. So people like me, we live in a modest home and fixed it up. Why should we bail out someone who bought a home in the suburbs that's twice the size of ours?"

And yet, Ostrowski believes that the bailouts are really only a prelude to the Debt Years to come - long-term economic stagnation fueled by large debt loads – a *Debtpression*, if you will. "It's really these subsidies. The explosion of debt. The inflation – the anticipated inflation which is going to happen to pay for all these things. And inflation will lead to social unrest at some point. At some point we're going to have to monetize all this debt and print more money, and that's going to jack up prices. People are going to say, *prices are too high.* You're going to have price-controls slapped down. That's going to lead to shortages. Shortages could lead to social unrest, not because of the market, but because of all the activities of the government. So we're very concerned if these impossible trends are allowed to continue, you're going to have civil unrest.

"Far from the notion of the *Tea Party people* being the crazy ones who want to engage in violence, we're the ones who are looking at the trends and saying, *My God, if we don't get our act together now, our country is going to fall apart,*" he says, his arms outstretched, as if to drive home the point. "We're the ones trying to save the country, and we're the ones getting smeared for it by the media. And you know what? It's not working. According to the latest polls, people are buying what we're selling."

What frustrates him, he seems to be saying, aren't the individual stories of people struggling to pay their bills in a time of economic instability, so much as his fear that the future might be far worse. "I think it was the $12 trillion transfer of wealth – the biggest bank robbery in the history of the human race performed by our government," he says, his voice strengthening to make his displeasure clear. "To me it was clear our government became a *kleptocracy*, a regime that steals - like a banana republic. And that couldn't be allowed to continue."

It's why the attorney fights for a return to the Constitution in American life. Then again, he thinks that going back to the Constitution may not be all it's cracked up to be because the truth is, the Constitution led us here. "The Constitution gave the government enough excuses on paper to create this monstrosity that we have now," he says. "And it's been interpreted and stretched and so on, but the language was there. So I think we need to go pre-Constitutional. We need to go back to the origins of this country. The origins were the Minutemen, the Declaration of Independence, the Articles of Confederation…I think the Constitution failed if it's purpose was to create limited government. I think we need to get back to quasi-independent states that are aligned for purposes of national defense and free trade because all libertarians believe in free trade – real free trade – not this crap we have now. We believe in real free trade. So that's the model that I propose."

Ostrowski says he often returns to the writings of the Founding Fathers, even those Founders who may have escaped the average American's grasp of history. In researching his book, *Direct Citizen Action*, he says he was reminded that "several of the most prominent people - I believe that includes Patrick Henry and George Mason - didn't sign the Constitution. Robert Yates is probably the greatest lawyer New York ever produced. He was known as Brutus, the anti-Federalist. He predicted accurately what would happen if the Constitution would get ratified." Very basically, Brutus argued that the newly created federal government would force the people to give up too much of their freedom. He believed that the citizens could never regain their power as the government took more and more from them over time. "He was a prophet," Ostrowski says. "We have to go back to origins. And the origin is to get back our liberty."

The attorney says the Tea Party gives him hope, if only because more and more people are realizing that their freedom can be lost. "We've got to get back to what the Minutemen were fighting for, which is the right to liberty," he says powerfully, almost as if he's suddenly inspired by the thought of Brutus. "And we've got to chop government way down to size…so if someone molests you in the course of your day when you're doing your business, the government can step in and solve that problem somehow. The rest of it, we don't need it. We don't need it. We don't need the government intervention. We don't need the *welfare state*. It's been a failure. It's hurt the people it was designed to help. We don't need the government involved in the economy. We don't even need the government's paper fiat money supply. The market will supply money as it always has."

Ostrowski has two children, ages eight and eleven. He sends them both to a private school. He obviously worries about their future, but that's one of the reasons he wrote his book which is full of ideas on how the average citizen can empower him or herself to change America. He argues that you don't even have to run for office or lobby the politicians. "Number one, take your kids out of the government schools. We are allowing the government to indoctrinate our kids into a false sense of history and a false sense of what our history is," he says. "Take them out. I know it's a sacrifice. I do it. It's a mortgage payment every month, but we do it.

"And there's a lot of things people can do. Stop buying – we believe in boycotting business firms that donate money to politicians. We believe in educating ourselves in the real history of the United States and economics - free market economics. If you're against socialism, that means you're for free-market economics. But do you *understand* free market economics? I mean, there's online materials at the Mises Institute, at Mises.org, that are fantastic in explaining these complicated things to people in a way they can understand. You don't have to be an economist to understand it."

He says it all starts with education. "Read the Declaration of Independence. It's all there. You have certain rights, and the government's job is to protect your rights and that's it. It's real simple. And all the attempts for the government to do more than that, they've all failed - every single one of them. Public housing projects – failure. Bringing democracy to any country around the world - it's all failed. Foreign aid – failed. All the things the government does that it should not be doing. Public schools are a massive failure. It's producing a generation of, unfortunately, mediocrity - and people who don't even know the history of their country. People can't even name what century the Civil War was fought in. I think you should be able to describe some of the key battles in the Civil War if you're an American. You should know what happened in day one, two, and three at Gettysburg. That stuff is important. And we're losing our heritage in this country."

Along with education, Ostrowski believes change comes through action. "Basically, applying what people like Gandhi and Martin Luther King did to this movement. And not always just trying to get someone elected or lobbying someone who's been elected. We've got to get more effective than that - way more effective." That's where he sees all the pent-up potential of the Tea Party leading – to action that could someday force change. It's a controversial path, and one that he admits would not be easy, especially as the movement struggles to find its identity.

He also admits real-life is never as easy as theory. I ask him if some of the critics might actually be right, that perhaps parts of the Tea Party could have been co-opted by special interests, potentially dealing a heavy blow to the "grassroots" feel of some of the movement. "There is an Astroturf aspect to the Tea Party movement," he says. "But you know what? It's also a decentralized, grassroots movement. I know it's like, maybe a little too complicated for Keith Olbermann to understand, but yes. There are some billionaires out there with phony groups claiming to run the Tea Party movement. That's true. But there's also a true Tea Party movement. We had 1,500 people the other day, and they're all local people. And we've never gotten any money from the Coke Foundation, so it's the real thing, folks. It's not fake."

Ostrowski sums it up like this: "The country is going down the drain, and we're going to be bankrupt. The economy is going to collapse, and we're going to have civil unrest. There's nothing that guarantees peace in the United States. Peace and civility are values that have to be fought for on a daily basis, just like war. You have to fight for peace. You have to fight for a society where there's *not* rioting in the streets. That's what we're fighting for now. We're not for that – we're fighting *against* that. Because we see that that may come in the future."

He warns that America's leaders had better pay attention. "We're what's happening," he says. "If they're not paying attention, then they're just going to get swept up in the tide of history. Because we're coming. We're going to win this fight - one way or the other - without violence and without any illegality. We're going to win."

Earlier, inside the appellate courtroom, Ostrowski asked the five justices to "breathe new life into the old and wise Constitution…and to breathe new life into the very notion of constitutionally limited government." In his prepared notes he posed this question: "For what good are constitutions if their plain language and clear intent are ignored and constitutions become mere props upon which false oaths are sworn by newly elected public officials?"

As the interview concludes, he says he isn't sure that the court will see "The Pork Lawsuit" as he does. He hints that the government has too much to lose if courts across the country started striking down the system as it stands.

In fact, only a few weeks later, the justices gave their ruling, and they agreed with Ostrowski and those who had argued that their tax money shouldn't be funneled to private corporations. It means there will be more legal battles ahead. In the end nothing may change. But with his arguments in court on that day, as well as his writings and daily actions, Ostrowski's voice – like thousands of others – is increasingly getting the chance to be heard.

Chapter III

The Sheriff

David Gergen (CNN senior political analyst): Republicans are "searching for their voice."

Anderson Cooper: "It's hard to talk when you're tea-bagging."

-CNN "Anderson Cooper 360"

April 15, 2009

At the Tea Party rally he was holding the new-age rebel flag - red and white stripes with a blue corner square. But in the corner, in place of the 50 stars symbolizing the 50 United States, the white stars encircled the roman numeral, *II*. In addition to the flag, Thomas Lorey wore a navy blue hat with *NRA* stitched on the front. Although he might not have stood out from the crowd of hundreds who waved flags and held the usual home-painted signs, it was startling to see the sheriff of a rural upstate New York county at such an event. Perhaps it shouldn't have been.

The sixty-two-year-old has been sheriff for 15 years in Fulton County. A few weeks after the rally, wearing his uniform with pockets full of the tools of his job, he shares his views on what he believes is a federal government run amok, an economy in shambles, and a society at the breaking point. Having to get elected to his position with his next bid set for 2011, I wondered if he were taking a risk by talking with me. "No," he replies in his gruff whisper of a voice. "I'm not taking a risk. I think that the majority of people I'm sworn to protect in Fulton County feel the same way I feel. If they don't feel that way, they don't have to vote me into office again."

He speaks confidently, occasionally leaning back in his office chair. His blonde hair and round, solid face gives him the look of someone younger, though his eyes give away the truth that he has often seen awful things throughout his years as sheriff. But it's his government job, ironically, that eventually lands him at one of the Tea Parties. "What I've seen is that the Constitution of the United States, written so many years ago, is not being followed," he says. "More and more, it's not being followed by the government that's in place today."

And that is a pretty big statement, given that he wears a badge to work each day. To many, he *is* the government. But as sheriff, he sees himself as a protector of the people. It seems he believes there is no conflict because he doesn't believe he is the one encroaching on people's lives. "I am part of the government," he admits. "I'm the first line of the government, if you will. I think people see me as *their* lawman. I'm their guy that people can elect, and they can fire me. I'm their boss. If I say the wrong thing, they're not going to like me. But I'm not saying things just so people like me. Obviously, you know what I truly believe in. I went to the Tea Party rally to give them my support."

Sheriff Lorey seriously considers for a moment what government is doing wrong. He says he "woke up" to a new way of thinking around 2005 after local and national events finally added up to a government that, in his opinion, had gone too far. "There's a couple things that strike me as being unconstitutional, but nobody's ever taken them to the lengths of appeals or anything," he says.

His first "pet peeve," as he puts it, are traffic laws. He brings it up to build a bridge to his larger points that already seem ready to bubble up from under the surface. So he starts with roadway infractions, the laws that lead to most people meeting his deputies. "Motorcycle helmets and seatbelts. I know that the intent is to keep accidents down, save injuries. That's all well and good. We have laws in place that protect children from being injured. We have an obligation to do that as human beings. When someone reaches the age of 21, I don't think the government needs to tell them that they need to wear a motorcycle helmet, that they need to buckle themselves up. Those are two things that they're only going to injure themselves. I wear a seatbelt because I believe in them. I would not ride a motorcycle without a helmet. They save lives. But I don't believe I should have to tell you how *you* can go about your everyday life. Those are the most glaring things I can think of, encountered by people everyday. People resent those laws."

Beyond traffic laws, the sheriff says that the people's Second Amendment right to keep and bear arms is often trampled by limitations placed on a person's ability to carry a concealed weapon. Along with a number of other states, Lorey says, "I think the state of New York has some extremely tough gun license rules (for) handgun permits. They're administered through sheriffs throughout the state. Let me give you an example you can use. I can go to the state of Pennsylvania and register for a handgun permit as a non-resident. I pay a fee, I get the permit. That permit is accepted by 21 other states." Lorey crosses his arms and leans forward in his chair, his voice low, but stern. "People have the right to defend themselves. New York State makes it so tough for people to get a permit. It's very costly in the first place, there are restrictions placed on them. They don't accept any other state's permit. If you have one in the state of Florida, (if) you move here and bring your gun here - even if you have a permit - you're guilty of a crime. I don't think that's right. Government is forcing itself too much into people's private lives."

And yet, there are those who think that guns should be outlawed altogether, believing that they can only cause harm. Any reporter will tell you about murders and shootings on which he or she has reported. Those stories involve talking with mothers and fathers grieving over their lost sons or daughters. Travel to any city, you'll meet people devastated by gun violence, even if most of those crimes are committed with illegally owned guns. "Isn't it about safety?" I ask the sheriff.

"Certainly there's a balance," he says. "We need common sense rules. These other states that allow concealed carry have common sense rules. If you're issued a permit and you violate the law, the law comes down on you, which it should. If you want a permit to protect yourself in your home, you should certainly be allowed to have that.

"There's a big National Rifle Association case going on against the City of Chicago right now. There's a case that just went through the Supreme Court against the city of Washington, D.C., our nation's capital. I think it's outrageous that the government can tell people not to protect themselves in their own homes," he says. Soon after we spoke, the Supreme Court came down with a 5-4 decision agreeing with Otis McDonald, the 76-year-old African American Democrat who wanted to legally keep a handgun in his home, though Chicago had written a law against doing just that. The Court's ruling means the 2nd Amendment right to bear arms is now considered a *fundamental* American right. In other words, legal experts say it means that the Bill of Rights actually applies to state and local laws. It also means countless local gun laws will likely be challenged in the coming years.

Lorey continues by saying that he thinks a deteriorating economy makes it even more important for people to be able to defend themselves. If some might think him a *Chicken Little*, Lorey worries he's more a political prophet. He says this: "In Ashtabula County, Ohio, due to budget constraints, they laid off half of their sheriff's office. National news," he says. The truth is, they forced more than half of the sheriff's office out of their jobs, according to local reports. "Fact - the county judge went on a media appeal telling people to arm themselves, to be ready to defend their property because the local government wasn't going to be capable of doing it for them. I'm not saying everyone should go join a militia somewhere. But you should certainly be ready to defend your family and your home and what possessions you have because if the economy collapses, it's going to get pretty difficult. It would be very difficult for law enforcement, no matter who they are, to cover all the bases."

But is economic collapse possible? After all, we're hearing about economic recovery now, or, at worst - a *double-dip recession*. Some are saying job growth seems tantalizingly close after months of hundreds of thousands of jobs being eliminated across the country. Aware of the tape recorder on his desk, he whispers a word that begins, "bull--." Then, he explains why he doubts any talk of an economic recovery. "You're hearing *recovery* from the Republican folks who have a lot of money and delve into the stock market - who say *recovery* because the stock market is improving. The stock market is run by politicians. Walk around in Fulton County. Go stop at a farm. See if they think we're recovering.

"My biggest fear is the state of the economy and the economy in general...New York State is so dysfunctional the people have no idea. It's a ridiculous system that doesn't work. My fear right now is that the economy is on the verge of total collapse. The Social Security system is out of money. What a catastrophic thing it would be if all the retired people who rely on that to live - what would happen? People would be forced - it would be survival of the fittest, a scary, scary thing.

"Some of the reasons the economy has gotten out of hand, I blame on the big picture of labor unions," he says. Though union leaders would argue organized labor is the only way to keep the few at the top from profiting off of the work of everyone else, Lorey doesn't see it that way, at least not any longer. "They were very necessary when they first came into being, but they've gotten so out of control with their benefits and their demands that it's impossible for a small person to do any kind of business in the United States," he says. "Your shirts and pants were probably made in China because no one can afford to make them in the United States. And that's all of our faults. We fell asleep at the wheel somehow. You know, democracy can only exist as long as the people don't know they can vote themselves these huge entitlements and spend the taxpayer dollars foolishly. No democracy has ever lasted longer than a couple hundred years."

That may be one of the reasons why he carried the flag of the Second Revolution at the Tea Party rally. And yet, does he really think America is at its end or in need of a revolution? "Me, I'm very fearful…I'm thinking of a Second Revolution at the polls. My prayers are that this is going to work at the polls and people are going to realize that they do have a voice, and they can make changes without violence. But on the other hand, if the economy eventually crashes completely, if Social Security checks cease to exist, people are going to go back to their primal instincts. It will be survival of the fittest. People will feed their families if they have to."

So how does he balance a belief in small government with a hope that people's Social Security checks keep coming? Beyond the obvious point that US citizens are forced to pay into the system, Sheriff Lorey speaks about a group of people living in the area who have lived far more simplistically. The Amish, he says, "are not involved in government. They're not involved in voting. They aren't involved in anything other than what they do. They're involved with survival, and they haven't changed the way they do business in 100 years, and they're not going to in the next 100." These days, he says, "You don't have but a handful of people that are able to can things, grow vegetables, live off the land."

He worries that those skills may be increasingly important in the years ahead. "I think the writing is on the wall…if you don't live under a rock, you'd understand that the economy is about to bite the dust. *You'd understand that things are not like anything else you've ever known in your life*," he says, his voice rising in tone to accentuate his point. "You'd understand that somewhere, there's got to be a change.

"I got to the point I am from the 15 years of being in this office and the complaints I've heard from my constituents and the unfair taxation I've seen from the federal government, the state government, even the county government. Taxes – people are taxed to death. I think it's a terrible thing that the United States of America – half of the residents, by a statistical study, don't pay income taxes. That makes us who (do) pay our taxes support the half that don't." According to the nonpartisan group, The Tax Foundation, Lorey actually isn't far off. The organization reports that just about five years ago, "a record 42.5 million Americans who filed a tax return (one-third of the 131 million returns filed last year) had no tax liability after they took advantage of their credits and deductions. Millions more paid next to nothing."[1] According to various sources and news outlets, the number has remained about the same since.

With that, the sheriff turns to the issue of illegal immigration. It had become the topic du jour for the political pundits on TV, especially after Arizona passed a law basically making it illegal to be in the southwestern state illegally. Critics of the legislation fear that it could lead to racial profiling. "We have immigration laws on the books, but we don't enforce them," the sheriff says. "The federal government has an arm of the government that's supposed to take care of illegal aliens. Illegal aliens are in small counties like this, employed by farms. Nobody does anything. They take food out of the mouths of Americans as far as I'm concerned." He says he believes Americans would do the jobs that illegal immigrants do, if given the chance.

After covering some of the most controversial topics in the current American conversation, it's time to find out where he thinks the Tea Party movement fits in. "I think it's a movement of everybody," he says. "I don't think it's going to spark a resurgence of popularity in the Republican Party or the Democratic Party. A lot of people today are independents…They don't have a party and are freethinkers.

"The voice of the Tea Party, if I understand it correctly, is not to create dissention by violence. It's not to create anything other than to get the Americans aware of what's going on and send them to the polls. You may or may not be aware, but you probably must know - voters just don't turn-out as they should. Voting is what can change everything. That's what the Tea Party is all about, getting people that are angry and using their frustration to put some new people in."

I ask Sheriff Lorey if he encountered any racists at the rally, or if he saw anyone who might have had violent intentions. Before he answers, he decides to take the media to task: "Mainstream media, all media, maybe yourself included, they have a tendency to sensationalize smaller incidents. The Tea Party has a bad rep. Some of the media zeroing in on some particular radical people prone to violence may have given the impression they're involved with the Tea Party…I think it's like

---

[1] Hodge, Scott A. "Number of Americans Outside the Income Tax System Continues to Grow." http://www.taxfoundation.org/research/show/542.html. 5 June 2005.

anything else - a few bad apples can spoil the barrel. There are some very radical, dangerous people in America. The Tea Party is not connected in any way with them. They don't want to be connected in any way with them. Some militant people were arrested in a neighboring state. They were very radical and had terrible plans. But they weren't connected with any other militia. Even the militia groups that arm themselves and are allegedly ready to defend when they have to defend, they don't want to be associated with any of that nastiness." Sheriff Lorey says he believes that there is, in fact, militia "activity" in Fulton County, though he's never been able to put his finger on it. He believes that it likely consists of folks who are preparing themselves in case the worst should happen. "I started hearing talk for years in the county," he says. "There may be a militia here, like a ghost."

If economic uncertainty and a growing government are the concerns that move Sheriff Lorey to protest, it's also his disillusionment with a society that has strayed from simpler times. "I'm peaceful about it," he says. "Everybody has a right to their view. Maybe my view is not the right view. Who knows? But it's the view I've chosen to take and defend. I think America was founded for people who want to be patriots, people who want to defend what we've always known. And I think we're losing what we've always known. I grew up in a happier, gentler, kinder time. I lived in a small town. Everybody knew each other and left their keys in their cars in their yards. The doors were always open. If you needed a pound of sugar and your neighbor wasn't home, you'd leave him a note, or leave him a dollar for the sugar and go borrow some - and they'd think nothing of it."

True, getting back to those days might be the bittersweet impossible dream of a man who has seen too much tragedy throughout his career - too many car crashes, too many criminals, and too many people on the worst days of their lives. But Lorey, like others who have come to the Tea Party movement, still doesn't think all is lost. At least, that's his hope. "If I had my way and the dream of the Tea Party was to fulfill itself on Election Day, they'd put some new people in office. The people that are there either can't - or are not - doing the job that the people put them there to do. And there are too many people who have come to realize that. Things are in a terrible state of affairs. Laying off schoolteachers at an unprecedented rate. If you can't take care of the youth, give them a proper education, then we're really failing everything," he says.

As his hope rests on the ballot box, he wants solutions – fast.. "I wish I could change the government. I wish I could consolidate the government. I wish we could make the government smaller. We have way too much government red tape. Things get bogged down. Change is slow, if ever. Too many hands spoil the soup - an old adage, but it's true."

Arms still crossed, Sheriff Lorey looks like a man frustrated that others have forced him into this position. "I would certainly characterize myself as angry," he says, speaking in shorter bursts now. "I have a duty to protect the people. I took an oath to enforce the rules of the Constitution."

And that's the catch. At what point do all the laws and regulations force him to take a stand based on his own beliefs? Is there one day when he would have to put down his badge, or say, *not in my county,* and then tell the federal government to get out? Without pausing for a second, in his matter-of-fact, powerful whisper, he explains, "If the federal government would come to Fulton County and do things that I think are unjust, I think I have a duty to the people that voted me into office to see that the federal government is not allowed to put upon the people that I protect on a day to day basis." He says he would only put down his badge "when the people who employ me vote me out of office." But he goes further. "Let's say there was an all-out rule to confiscate everyone's firearm. I wouldn't participate. I would refuse to enforce that law, wherever it would take me. If the federal government chooses to put me in prison, so be it."

If there is one thing Lorey wants people to know, it's to have faith in your sheriff. "I think you'll find that your sheriff in your county feels the same way that I do. And your sheriff is going to be the last person standing as far as government and as far as your protection from evils in the world."

With that, Lorey pulls out miniature copies of the Bible and the Constitution, both of which he keeps in his uniform's right shirt pocket. In his other pocket, resting over his heart, he keeps a copy of The Declaration of Independence. "This is where I stand," he says. "I'm a patriot first and an American. I am a sheriff second."

Chapter IV

The Entrepreneur

"There's nothing more interesting than seeing a bunch of racists become confused and angry at a speech…Let's be very honest about what this is about. This is not about bashing Democrats. It's not about taxes. They have no idea what the Boston Tea Party was about. They don't know their history at all. This is about hating a black man in the White House. This is racism straight up. That is nothing but a bunch of tea-bagging rednecks. And there is no way around that…it is a neurological problem that we're dealing with."

-Janeane Garofalo, Activist/Comedian

April 15, 2009

Interview on "Countdown with Keith Olbermann"

At a gathering like so many across the country, Tea Partiers shiver from the cold, wet air. Bright yellow Gadsden Flags wave in the brisk wind. The fabric droops to the ground, weighed down by the heavy rain that just soaked the thousand or so people who filled the upstate New York amphitheater before the rally even began. They all braved the weather and the brief onslaught of pea-sized hail to attend the protest. Now, under the threatening clouds and out of the sound system come voices yelling, "freedom," over and over again. Others talk about realizing how they aren't alone. They speak of the surprise they feel once they figure out that others also believe the government has become too large and out of control.

Most who attend the rally sit on the concrete steps. They hold soaked signs painted with political slogans like *Taxed Enough Already*. On the far corner a group stands underneath a large tree, as if looking for some sort of shelter from the storm but not ready to give in and go home.

From 100 feet away you can't miss Earl Wallace as he stands underneath that tree. The well built, middle-aged man looks like he might have just dismounted from a horse that transported him from the 1700's. Yes, he's the guy wearing the full costume, harking back to the uncertainty, fear, and hope that surely filled the hearts and minds of the Colonists during the Revolution. Even his black shoes look like they were cobbled in another century. His dark vest, embroidered with gold, partially covers a frilly white shirt. Of course, he also wears the tri-corner hat that, until recently, had been relegated to those who spend their spare time re-enacting war scenes.

Wallace talks about the battles he has faced in his own life and how memories from nearly a lifetime ago shape his thinking today. "My mom was an amazing woman," he says. "But my mom, she had seven children, five out of wedlock by four different men." The costume seems to melt away as he speaks. His voice sounds so earnest, so serious, while his eyes hide behind dark sunglasses. "We were raised very poor because my biological dad was an alcoholic. I saw him maybe once between the ages of five and ten. We were a very poor family. But my mom was one of the co-founders of the Saratoga Springs Emergency Corps. Despite being poor, she still believed in doing what is right for the community."

Throughout our conversation, it's clear that Wallace feels he owes a debt to his mother for the lessons she taught him, lessons that brought him here today. "I see the value system which my mother instilled in me was really the value system from the Founding Fathers which is embedded in the Bill of Rights, which is really founded upon the Ten Commandments. The Founding Fathers realized through the Ten Commandments (that) God is saying, *you have a right not to be murdered. You have a right not to be lied to. You have a right to have your property and not to have your property seized.*" While he continues to mention his mother, he sounds almost like a textbook on Thomas Jefferson at the same time. "There are the due process rights that have evolved in America where citizens have the opportunity to achieve in a free, pluralistic society, where you have to weigh one person's rights to do something with another person's right *not* to have it done to them." He thinks that somewhere along the way, the American government had overstepped its bounds.

Wallace says it took him years to come around to such thinking. His voice grows deeper and more serious as he explains how his mother tried to make an impression on him decades ago. "In 1967 when welfare legislation was passed - when the Great Society legislation was passed - my mother told me this would be the single-worst thing that could happen to African-American people. I'm an African-American, obviously, and I argued with her. I said, 'Mom, people need the support.' And she went up and down our block and pointed to different households. She said, 'Do you see this person is the assistant to the vice president of a particular company? This person is the head welder in his company.' And she said if you hear these people talk, you will realize they've been called *nigger* on the job. Every one of these people have been called *nigger* on the job, but they didn't let that stop them. They persevered - just like the Jews had to persevere, just like the Irish had to persevere, just like the Italians and the German immigrants had to persevere. And if you have welfare, it is going to fracture families. It is going to encourage and compel people to not put up with the hassles of what it takes to achieve in America."

Wallace says that for years he remained unconvinced by his mother's arguments. He challenged her, arguing that without the government, some would have nothing and that there could never be a level playing field without government help. Back in his college days, he says he even referred to himself as a "flaming liberal." But over time, his great hope in the Great Society policies and the growing government began to dissipate like the storm that had just soaked the Tea Party rally. He began to think that, perhaps, government wasn't the answer to everything. It was a thought that shook his political soul. The older he became, the more he believed that individuals with a clear focus could support each other and accomplish more than the broad hand of the government. Wallace illustrates his point with a memory from years ago: "there was a Nazi that came into town, (along with) the Ku Klux Klan." He says that they held meetings at a local hotel, and many in the black community took the visit as a serious threat. "Many of my white friends called me up and said, 'I have a gun for each one of the windows in your house. Where do you want me?' We don't tolerate this in our community."

I ask him what he thinks about the Tea Party media coverage. Protesters around the country have been accused of carrying racially insensitive signs and shouting racial slurs. The national commentators quickly latched on, leveling the accusation that the Tea Parties stemmed from white anger, that the rallies might be nothing more than a reaction to the first black president. Wallace begins his answer by explaining that there seems to be a lot of miscommunication going on in America. Politicians don't seem to want to actually solve the problems that an increasingly vocal American population wants solved, he says. He thinks that is what stirred up the rallies, not racial hatred. "These issues are very simple," he says. What you (leaders) want to do is to hide behind the complications, the smokescreen, so that when we do dissect what (you're) saying, you can say, 'Oh it's complicated,' and run off with an argument that doesn't make sense to us."

Moreover, Wallace says the idea that the Tea Parties are gatherings of racists simply misses the point: "Unless I'm directly calling you a name, how can (you) level that charge?" he asks. For Wallace, race just isn't the big issue. "I'm married to a white woman and my children are mixed race. My wife and I adopted a mixed-race child who is married today to another adopted child out of South America. We *are* the melting pot. I have dogs and cats – they're all mutts. We're all mutts. We're enjoying the American way of life. Some of my wife's cousins are here with me today as a matter of fact." He says he has never felt uncomfortable at a rally. He puts it simply - just because he has a different political view, it doesn't make him a racist. "I have people that disagree with *me* because I'm an African-American conservative," he says.

Wallace moves the conversation from race to religion. He believes that the more the country moves away from its Judeo-Christian roots, the more America will struggle to find harmony. It's a common concern among many at the Tea Parties. "When I was raised, my mother taught me that America was a melting pot and that you could come here and be an American, and if you throw out the value system, then you throw out the behaviors that have brought us where we are."

However, the topic that Wallace keeps coming back to isn't race or religion - but America's future. He even hints that he believes America is sliding toward socialism or communism. "I don't admire Hugo Chavez. I don't admire Fidel Castro. Mao Zedong and Hitler were enemies of mankind as was Josef Stalin," he says, arguing that if the US is moving towards such systems – it should stop.

So where does Wallace think America went wrong? "I don't believe that we should be aborting babies. I believe we should be a people that give life. We should be a people who embrace life…I was raised in a fatherless home. I was a poor child. I have a master's degree today. I am an author of a book. It's on *Amazon.com*. Many people that I was raised with are in prison today. But some of us thought differently. Some of us didn't blame *the man* for our problems. We realized if you do certain things, certain things will happen to you. And our government needs to realize that if you over-regulate things, you're going to kill them."

He continues to talk about over-regulation and says that if it's enacted, the *value-added tax* or *VAT*, could further cripple the American economy. The VAT is a tax common in European nations, allowing national governments to tax the added market value of a product at various stages of the product's path to the consumer. It's something that many Tea Party ralliers mention because they fear it will be in America's future, possibly sold to the public as a way to pay down the exploding debt. They believe that many Americans might even support the tax since they might be told that *they* don't actually pay it, the *producers* do, though critics argue that the cost is simply passed on to consumers. Wallace believes the VAT, like so many current government policies, would only stifle American progress. "We want our country to be focused on creating a set of circumstances that are reasonable for reasonable people to succeed at what they choose to succeed at, providing it's not breaking the law," he says.

"Government today is suffering from a lack of vision," he continues. "They don't understand that government was founded really as a government that supports a free capitalistic system so that people in America can use their creativity and their ingenuity to innovate and provide goods and services that people are willing to pay for. We share the fruits of that with employees and partners in terms of salaries and benefits. That's the foundation of the American system.

"The challenge we have today…government is getting away from the main mission. The mission of government is to create a set of favorable circumstances so *we, the people,* can succeed with our lives. Americans want to reach for the stars. We don't want to have a system that regulates us to making sure we just don't hit the ground. And as government overreaches its main mission, it keeps creating policies that have unintended consequences." The unintended consequences? Wallace points to corruption as one example. "There's a lot of fraud," he says. "Our government has told us repeatedly, *let's pass healthcare legislation and we'll clean up Medicare and Medicaid fraud.* I say prove it by cleaning it up now."

After sharing his biggest political fears, Wallace ponders what the Tea Party movement is truly all about. "I am hoping that it means – I want to say, *give me liberty or give me death*, but people will misinterpret that statement. I believe people get choked when they do not have opportunity. When government subsidizes, it tends to discourage. Once the activity gets so unproductive that it stops moving, then government wants to subsidize it. And I think our challenge today is that - our money system. Money is like oxygen for a fire. And the more government sucks the oxygen out of the system, the less there's going to be for a private citizen to actuate their lives. As a private citizen, as a businessperson, and as an author and entrepreneur - and as a person who's worked in state government for a very long time before this - I always felt that our role in government was to serve the public, not to dictate to the public, not to control the public. Government needs to balance some things in the private sector so people do have the opportunity to achieve and so one person's not taking advantage of another. But government is selling itself to the highest bidder, and they're doing it in the name of helping poor people, and they're doing so in the name of democracy."

While Wallace's voice sounds full of concern, somehow, it still radiates with the feeling that brighter days must be ahead - with Tea Parties paving the way. "I'm hoping it doesn't end, that the momentum carries through to the November elections," he says. "I'm hoping that, what I'd like to call, *the principles upon which America was founded*, prevail in the political arena and that the people elected in November are a reflection of that. I've been to a lot of meetings, and the people here don't want to be called Republicans. They don't want to be called Conservatives. They don't want to be called the Tea Party movement, either. They just want to be known as people who believe in American values. And we want to preserve that for our children and our grandchildren."

Wallace, like many of the others, seems to believe that the window of opportunity to "fix" America may be smaller than most people realize. He speaks with a sense of urgency, worrying that what he sees as the government's missteps could soon overwhelm society. And that, he believes, could deny his grandchildren a lifestyle of their choosing. "When I saw the debt – I think it's $31,000 and change per household – I looked at my grandchildren and thought, *I have to do something*. This is not what parents do for their children. It's what irresponsible parents do to their children. It's what alcoholic parents and drug addicted parents do to their children. As reasonable Americans, we aspire to more than that for our children and our grandchildren. I have four grandchildren, and a fifth one will be born in June. I'm hoping to leave them a better place than the direction of where we're headed."

After all, he doesn't want to leave his grandchildren the remnants of the recent economic storm. So now, he takes shelter in the ideals of the Tea Party. He carries with him the lessons he learned from his mother, lessons that he now shares with anyone who is willing to listen because he is sure his family's future depends on it.

Chapter V

The Retirees

"Most Americans who don't like Obama or the health care bill are not racists. It may be a closer call among Tea Partiers, of whom only 1 percent are black, according to last week's much dissected Times/CBS News poll.. That same survey found that 52 percent of Tea Party followers feel "too much" has been made of the problems facing black people — nearly twice the national average. And that's just those who admit to it. Whatever their number, those who are threatened and enraged by the new Obama order are volatile."

-Frank Rich

April 17, 2010

"Welcome to Confederate History Month"

New York Times Op-Ed

Out of hundreds and hundreds of people carrying signs, waving the flag of the Second American Revolution or other versions of the Stars and Stripes - Michael and Gigi Koen stand out. They hold up hand-painted signs like most of the others, but something intangible forces your eyes to collide with theirs. Perhaps their age is part of the reason; Gigi is 72-years-old, and Michael 70. Most protesters at this Tea Party are 30 to 40 years younger.

Others, as usual, hold handmade signs that read, *End the Fed*, *Impeach Obama*, and, *Your Healthcare is Making Me Sick*. The Koens are a team effort; one hoists a sign into the air that reads, "Oh Yes We Can." The other holds the reply, "Oh No You Can't," an obvious play on President Obama's campaign rhetoric, and, they joke, a hint at a few spousal conversations they've had over the years. "Well, we have to have an entrance," says Michael. "If you're going to a rally, you got to have signs. We started off rather timidly."

But if their signs indicate that they are having fun at their first real political rally, the Koens still created them to make a point. They want to be seen, to have a voice in the midst of a large mass of people. Ask them, and they will talk for hours about some of the times they have lived through. As compared to some of Gigi's childhood experiences, it seems this rally is quite enjoyable for her. The Tea Party, they both figure, is a fitting location for them to blow off a little steam.

For Gigi, it's a life story that certainly doesn't begin anywhere close to the upstate New York Tea Party. Nor does it begin in America because she wasn't even born here. "I grew up in Schlesia," Gigi says, her thick German accent punctuated by her thinning blonde hair bouncing up and down. "Right on the Polish border. It used to be a fight between Poland and Germany." Gigi was only seven-years-old by the time World War II had reached into every European's life.

"The Russians pushed the Polish people down, and the Polish people were pushed into Schlesia - and we were pushed out. We had to go on a train," Gigi says, without giving away how dire her family must have known the situation to be. She gives no clue that it's a miracle she is here in the United States retelling her story. With her father away at war fighting for the Germans, survival in the mid-1940's depended on her grandmother, mother, brother, and little sister.

Gigi remembers turning seven-years-old very well. "On my birthday, yeah. I had to leave all my birthday presents behind," she says. "At 11 o'clock at night, the loudspeakers came on and said, *We cannot hold the city, the Russians will be here by the morning. Please leave in an orderly fashion. And go to the train station and get your ticket. Get on the train and get out. Don't pack any suitcases. Just leave the way you are. You will be returned in a day or two.*" The war in Europe still raged, but the German Empire had already started to cave in on itself.

Gigi and her family rushed to the closest train station. "They were the last train," her husband explains. "You had like a half-hour to get your things together and get your ticket -" Before he finishes, Gigi takes over the thought.

"- Because the Russians were fighting outside the city," she continues. "So we got to the train station, and our house was right across from the main post office. It was bombed, it blew all up. So we knew we didn't have anything left."

Gigi's family members were prepared for the evacuation, just in case. "We got on the train, and we were the third car. (What had been) the last car had been shot off. Someone went and unhooked the car on fire," Gigi says, her eyes clearly seeing the flames that burned 65 years ago. "Then we were in the last one by the time we got out of the city. So we were on the train…and we slept on the baggage nets and once a day, the train stopped. They used the water from the steam engine and gave us a little cup with dry milk and a little piece of dry bread and that's what we ate. We were on the train for a month." The train took them through Czechoslovakia and Bohemia, from Bohemia to Bavaria. "And they disconnected a cart on each city and that's where we were deposited," she says.

What was she, a seven-year-old girl, thinking during this time? If Gigi was frightened while her world irrevocably changed, she clearly doesn't remember it that way. "You just go with the flow you know? I jumped on the trucks," she says. The Americans had come through with their tanks by this time. "I knew exactly when the Americans went in their chow lines," Gigi laughs. "So friends and I went and jumped on the trucks just to have food."

Her new life in Bavaria was far different than what most Americans could even begin to imagine, given the current digital immediacy of almost everything we're familiar with in the 21st century. But back then, just getting food was a multi-step process. "After the fields were cleared, we refugees were allowed to pick the bundles of wheat," she says matter-of-factly. "We would collect it and go from one village to the other and go to the mill to have it ground into flour. And you would give the flour to the baker, and the baker would give us a loaf of bread in exchange. And we had to walk five or four miles home."

She remembers that her trips to obtain life-sustaining bread could have been deadly. "Well, the thing was, we were not allowed to go on the railroad tracks because Americans were coming in with their planes and shooting the railroad tracks to get rid of the infrastructure. But when we went on a shortcut through the woods, there was illegal butchering going on, and we were chased by the illegal butchers with their knives. So we were darned if we did and darned if we didn't," explains Gigi, actually laughing at the thought. She says her group decided it was safer to risk getting shot at by the American planes than it was to risk running into the butchers. "We were about five kids on the railroad tracks. We saw the plane come in - we jumped in the ditch, held our heads, and the bullets went around us, and as soon as the plane was gone we were back on the tracks. And that was unbelievable – about six or eight times each trip we had to jump in the ditch and the bullets went around us because they had orders to shoot anything that was moving. Well, if you're in a plane like this, you can't see if it's kids or people. I was shot at so many times, it just became a game. We thought it was funny. We came home and said, how many times did you count the bullets went around us?" The planes, the bullets, getting bread - it was just the way life was. "We were so hungry. If we would have taken a bite out of the bread, our mother or grandmother would have killed us. So here we were walking to the mill, walking to the baker, having a little knapsack, putting the bread in there - getting shot at."

Gigi's improbable presence at a Tea Party rally in America more than 60 years later still seemed far from likely at the time, but a few years later, she attended college in England. Michael, who was in the service, was sent to Europe from 1957 to 1960 and was happy to simply speak English with this young German woman whom he had just met. "It took a lot of nerve to walk over on the dance floor and ask someone to dance, never knowing what to expect," Michael says. He laughs, "It went pretty good."

Gigi picks up the story from there: "He asked me to dance, and I said, 'Yup.' He said, 'You speak English?' I said, 'Yup.' I was a woman of a lot of words, but all I could say was 'Yup.' We kind of liked each other, but it took a while. It took about a year. He said to me, 'Will you visit or let me know when I could come over?' He got very anxious and had his father sponsor me."

Michael wants to talk immigration as he remembers the difficulty in getting the immigration system to allow his future wife to stay in America. But Gigi continues with her story, talking about her first impression of America. "I was in New York City. I hated the city. I was a girl from a small town. I landed smack (in the) middle of Harlem. What did I know about Harlem coming from Germany?" She says she arrived at her first apartment and saw seven locks on the front door. "I thought, 'Oh my God. Where did I land?' And then I was in a room and the mattress was like a camel's back. There was an old radio in there. The problem was that the building was like a horseshoe and the fellow across could see me getting undressed, so I had to go down in front of the window."

Gigi says trying to stay in America with all the proper forms and clearances was a tedious process, as almost any naturalized citizen will tell you. She will also tell you that it's one of the reasons illegal immigration to the United States bothers her so much. She makes it clear she's not anti-immigration, but anti-*illegal* immigration. After all, she became a citizen after completing the arduous immigration process herself. "I was one. But make it legal," she says. "It took me quite awhile. I had to have a sponsor. I was on a list. There were quotas. Each country had a quota, and you could only let so many immigrants come in - so many from France, so many from Germany, and all the different countries."

Michael explains, "You had to wait almost a year to get her on that immigrant status list and be granted a visa to come."

"Then I had to (go to the) American Consulate and be interviewed about my political views," Gigi says. "If I was pregnant, I had to be examined. It was horrible. And it was degrading to go through all that trying to come here - five years to become a citizen. Then I had to take a test in English. I opened my pocketbook, I closed my pocketbook. I go upstairs, I go downstairs. I said, 'Come on you guys, what do you think, I'm an imbecile?' But what really gets me is as soon as they come over the border, illegal, they apply for welfare, for Medicaid. The next day they can go to vote. And within a week they are completely integrated," she says.

True, it is a federal crime for illegal immigrants to vote, but numerous sources argue that in practice, if a person can sneak through the system, they can then use their voter registration information to obtain other benefits. But to what extent illegal immigrants have done it or continue to do it, is unclear. It's something that's often emotionally debated by many so-called experts.

Gigi continues, each word painted by her German accent: "And they don't even have to learn the language. Now *we* have to learn Spanish in order to communicate with them, you know? It just doesn't make sense." Michael adds that he doesn't like how some countries allow for dual citizenship. He feels it can lead to a conflict of loyalty.

There would be no concerns about allegiance for Gigi, who eagerly assimilated into American life. "I like the country," she says. After initially coming to America for only two years, "I've been here ever since – 50 years. I like it because it's a free country. You don't have to walk the line like a herd of cattle. There's more freedom to move. It's just a different atmosphere. That's what I like about the country. And now we are going the way Europe has. And soon we will have 75% of our earnings taken away. You know, *we can't handle money, we are too dumb to know how to spend our own money*. I don't like that."

She says that she is even more concerned about the *processes* that are being used to pass legislation in Congress. Like others at Tea Party rallies, Gigi blames "Pelosi" and "Reid." Michael finishes his wife's thought about people's earnings being taxed, worried about the Value Added Tax, or VAT, paid by producers each step of the way as value is added to a product on its way to market. "I don't want to be doom and gloom," Michael says, "but – now they're saying we can (pay for the US debt) with a value added tax. In Denmark for instance, they're -"

"- 75 percent," Gigi chimes in.

"They started at seven percent and now they're up to a value added tax of 25 percent," Michael says. "Then they have the income tax. The total income is 75% tax for the average Danish person." Different mathematical formulas give different average tax rates, but the Danish income tax is around 60%, with a 25% sales tax.[1] Gigi wonders why anyone there would even go to work. Michael fears that the US is headed towards the European style-system too. "Yeah why go to work, you know?"

It's not just Europe's taxes, but also Europe's healthcare system that the Koens worry about. They fear it's the model America will soon adopt. And they'll tell you that they believe they have insight into the healthcare debate since they say they've come to know America's healthcare system too well. "It was a fluke," Michael says, insisting that he relay the story of just how they came to know the world of insurance, co-pays, bills, and yes – treatment. "The whole thing started - we were riding our bicycles ten to fifteen miles down on the bike path and one day there was a crossing that no one ever paid attention to. No one stopped. We could see left and right. One day a truck came along for the water-company." He and his wife collided as they tried to avoid the water truck, "and she fell off into a patch of poison ivy. We didn't have insurance so we had to go to one of these little clinics they have around to get the salves and lotions and what not. It just didn't go away. We tried everything - oatmeal baths and you name it - every ointment there was on the market. And no one wanted to take us because we didn't have insurance."

"They didn't want us paying for it either," Gigi says, shocked at the Catch-22 they found themselves in.

---

[1] "Denmark Tax Rates." http://www.taxrates.cc/html/denmark-tax-rates.html.

See also: "High income taxes in Denmark worsen a labor shortage," by Carter Dougherty. The New York Times. December 5, 2007. (cont'd)http://www.nytimes.com/2007/12/05/business/worldbusiness/05iht-labor.4.8603880.html

"We couldn't break down the barrier," Michael continues. "Couldn't get past the barrier with the receptionist. They would invariably say, *we're not taking any new patients.*" Then, Gigi says, the receptionist would inquire about what insurance they had. But they didn't have any; the Koens were willing to pay cash, insurance or not. Michael says they were repeatedly told the doctor didn't take cash. "And if you needed a (specialist), *oh well, we have an opening in October.* But we needed help right away."

Gigi's medical condition was plain as day to see, with blisters all over her body. "I mean, I looked like the monster-man from top to bottom," she says. "Unbelievable."

"Finally, we got to see a doctor and he gave a full exam, and they found a lump. *This is suspicious,*" Michael says, mimicking the doctor. "So they had a mammogram and a sonogram and sure enough, it had just started a month before. So if we hadn't fallen in that patch of poison ivy, who knows? You can talk about divine intervention."

But there didn't seem to be much divine intervention when it came to paying for all the treatments that Gigi required. The couple obtained health insurance only to find a maze of rules and payment structures that were both bewildering and costly. "If you have (a bill for) $2,500, the insurance will pay - and then you have to pay the next $2,500 yourself, or $4,000. And the drugs are out of reach," she says, her voice getting louder. "And that's another problem. Why can we get drugs cheaper from Canada? Why do we have to pay double here? I just cannot believe that. We get our Social Security, so right away they take away $100 from his, from mine. And then we have to pay on top of our own insurance premiums another $200. So actually, we pay $400 and we used to pay that when we were employed. It's not a free ride."

Michael predicts that it's only a matter of time before their Medicaid Advantage costs rise, probably by several hundred dollars a month. Gigi is frustrated: "Then we have to have all these co-pays. I had 32 radiations. I had to pay 32 times $12. For the chemo I had very, very expensive drugs because my white blood cells dropped. Those were $140 a shot. And things like that - it's not affordable." Gigi decides to throw gasoline on the political fire: "You get an illegal alien in here, and they get it free."

They do agree that reform is necessary, but they don't see the right reform in the recently passed *reform bill* that they view as a step toward socialized medicine. "We're all for reform, but we don't like how they crammed that through," he says. "There was no *take it or leave it*, it was just *take it. You're taking it whether you want it or not.*"

"We didn't count on cancer," Gigi says. "We were sailing along beautifully. I was never sick when I paid for my insurance at GE (or) when we paid our insurance while self-employed. Never took a sick day. Now all of a sudden you get hit over the head and it's terrible. You have to decide if you're going to eat or if you're going to buy the expensive drug. I had an antibiotic that was $460. I mean, come on. Give me a break."

The expensive drugs did their trick, though. Five years later, Gigi is cancer free. "I'm doing well," she says. "I never complained about the cancer. I talk to people in the treatment room." She smiles as she explains how she encourages other cancer patients to be strong. When they're scared, when they haven't been through what she has, "I say, *It's intimidating, those big machines. You just close your eyes, lay down, do what the girls tell you. Nothing is going to happen to you.* The same with chemo. I made fun of it. I had a wig and I went around just shaking it. I was a clown in chemo."

She laughs again, brushing cancer aside just like that - with medicine and the best medicine of all. But both Gigi and her husband turn serious when they start talking about how they fear the US could also be heading toward a European-style healthcare system. Michael interjects that he wishes tort reform had been added to the recent reform legislation too. Tort reform, of course, is legislation that would change the law as to how people are able to obtain compensation for damages. It would also impact how much money a person suing a doctor might receive. Although it may be a drop of water compared to the ocean of healthcare costs, Michael argues that its ripple could still have an impact. "That should have been included because in Europe you can't sue a doctor. They have socialized medicine, and you just can't (do it). It's all government healthcare."

The thought of government healthcare scares Michael, especially after the stories that the two have heard from their friends in Europe. "I've seen it over there," he says. "I've been in some healthcare facilities over there, and what you have, basically, is mass-hypochondria. If you know it's free, everybody goes if it's a little hangnail…So it's very expensive. Very expensive."

Gigi emphatically explains that in her opinion, the European approach has been awful for her family members she left behind. "You see, the communication lines are not there," she says. "My mother was ill, and she could only tolerate so much – 30 milligrams of cortisone. She was readmitted to another doctor who gave her 130 milligrams of medication and she died. That wouldn't happen here in the United States...I called up a doctor in the hospital and he said, *just pray your mother died fast.* I said to him, 'Did the neurology department request the previous findings and the file?' He said he'd call back, and, when he did, he said *no - - no request for the files.* So that would have been a lawsuit here." But it wasn't a lawsuit in Germany, where she says the problem occurred. Lawsuits might be expensive, but at least they allow for some sort of recourse, she argues. "And the same thing - my brother died at age 67. The doctor said, *oh yeah, I forgot to tell him he had two mild heart attacks.* The third one came and mowed him down. I mean, it was after he died, they did an investigation. The doctor said it never came up to tell him he had two mild heart attacks. It would have been a lawsuit here. My sister needs a new hip. She's been waiting for two years." Gigi says her sister will have to continue to wait until the government decides it's necessary. "And she's in pain. We are really concerned about the healthcare system. I wouldn't want to have socialized medicine here. It doesn't work."

But what about those who argue that everyone should have healthcare? "You have it," Michael says, agitated about the whole idea. "No one will get turned away."

But on reflection, it wasn't so much the VAT, or even the Koens' experience with the healthcare system, so much as their concern for the *overall* American system that gets them fired up. Like others who came to the rally, they worry that the US government is growing out of control and that the America Michael grew up in, the country Gigi emigrated to, is in danger. "The Tea Party has its connotations as a revolt against taxes," Michael says. "But it brought forth people like ourselves concerned with other issues. Primarily, it had all to do with an umbrella concern that government is too darn large."

Gigi continues, picking up the conversation from where her husband ended without a pause. "What really bothered me is the mandates, you know? We are 70 and 72 years old. We don't need to be treated like little children or like dummies. We have lived. We've been around the block. Why not give us the (credit) that we are grown up, we can make up our own minds? We have accomplished something in our lives. Please don't treat us like two-year-olds."

They may be critical of bigger government, but they also understand the dilemma that since they've paid into the Social Security system, for instance, they now rely on the government too. "Being older, the older generation, we paid for fifty years," says Gigi. "All of a sudden, we get Social Security and we're freeloaders. We don't count. So that kind of got us into the Tea Party movement. Nobody will listen to the older people. We're a bunch of old fogies. And it doesn't sit right." Bottom line, they both agree that they just don't feel like their voices have been heard as the politicians continue to bicker in Washington.

And then Michael says that although they're registered Republicans, they were honestly optimistic about the *change* promised in the 2008 presidential election. "We actually had great hopes for this administration," he admits. It's the sort of thing few people at Tea Party rallies are willing to talk about. "The rhetoric really sounded like there might be something new in this *change* policy, but the *change* that seemed to occur is really extreme."

They want term limits for politicians and hope the next several elections send a message. They want voters to shake things up, to put leaders on notice. "Gee, I hope we get some good politicians and lawmakers – a new breed of integrity and honesty," Michael says. It's a big reason that they both enjoyed attending the Tea Party rally. As they share pictures of themselves holding the two signs they carried at the protest, you can tell they feel a little rebellious about the whole experience, like teenagers trying to push the limits without getting grounded. Still, Michael says, "I wouldn't jump in a car and drive to Washington, as much as I'd like to. That's a little extreme for us."

Michael says the best part about going to their local rally was finding that they weren't alone in their shared political viewpoint. "We talked to a lot of people when we went down there, and a lot of people were thinking the way we were. We said smaller government, healthcare reform – to a point - and laws about illegal immigration."

Gigi herself had survived World War II in Europe. Against all odds, she came to America after meeting Michael. More than six decades later, after laughing at cancer, even after creating silly signs to take to the Tea Party rally, they turn deadly serious when it comes to their view of America's future. "I don't see much light at the end of the tunnel," Michael says. "I'm not looking for someone to ride in with a white horse and save the day, but you would think about the trillions of dollars we're in debt to China for, it would seem there is no end in sight or good outcome to this." He looks down at the ground, his head in his hands. "We gave up chasing rainbows a long time ago, but you've got to be hopeful that someone with more wisdom than us will come in and save the day. I don't think it's this administration, though. Honestly, I don't."

Chapter VI

The Tea Party Engineer

"What they want is the continuation of the failed economic policies of President George Bush which got us in the situation we're in now. What we want is a new direction…This initiative is funded by the high-end. We call it Astroturf. It's not really a grassroots movement. It's Astroturf by some of the wealthiest people in America to keep the focus on tax cuts for the rich instead of for the great middle class."

-House Speaker Nancy Pelosi

April 15, 2009

Interview on KTVU

Only a little while ago, Wade Abbott would not have understood what you were talking about if you had put the words *Tea Party* and *rally* in the same sentence. "A year-and-a-half-ago, I would have thought that's what the little girls do with their stuffed animals around the table," he says. He doesn't laugh when he says it because he's a pretty straightforward guy. "You know, I never saw myself as a political activist. Back in late 2008, the extent of my political involvement was simply going to the voting booth as a relatively informed voter. But I did listen to a lot of talk radio. I tried to keep up on the issues online, newspapers - things like that. I just found myself getting more and more fed up with the government."

During the tail end of the Bush administration, the 37-year-old father of two felt his anger solidify as he paid attention to the political scene. "We had the TARP (Troubled Asset Relief Program) bailouts that came to fruition in that timeframe," he says. "And then, after that, when President Obama was elected - the stimulus plan." But it wasn't only the national issues. Abbott grew even more concerned about some of the local tax plans, like a proposal that would tax sodas. The goal? To reward healthy decisions and fight obesity (many health experts believe that obesity is linked to high rates of soda consumption), and use the money raised from the tax to fund healthcare initiatives. "They started talking about the soda tax and all these other fees and taxes that were going to go up. My head just started spinning, and I was absolutely incensed," he says. Similar scenarios were playing out in states across the country, and arguably, in Western nations around the world.

Meanwhile, Abbott's newfound political ideals became even more entrenched as he faced a number of personal setbacks. "2009 (had) been a very interesting year," he says, his dark eyes looking through glasses as he pats down his short, dark hair that's combed forward. "It was a year of ups and downs. I had the Tea Party early on. I was an engineer working locally. Discovered it was a lot of hours, a lot of time put into the Tea Party." Abbott and his wife had planned on her being the one to stay home with their two children while he worked. "That was our game plan all along," he says. "She was going to stay home until the youngest got to be at least a year old. Then in May, I ended up losing my job. Things kind of got thrown into an uproar. It went from being a really great year, to, in some regards, one of the most challenging and difficult years."

Abbott decided to go back to school and work towards a master's degree in public communications, thinking that might be more in line with his goals than his materials engineering degree, especially since he began writing speeches. Although he'll tell you that he always hated writing in his past life, "I wanted to get some frustration off my chest." Writing his first political speech got him thinking - what would happen if others thought like he did? What if others wanted to vent their anger too? "We finally decided to hold (a rally) on April 1st. We thought, *what better day than April Fool's Day to beat up on the politicians.* This was - I believe this was late February, maybe even early March of 2009.

Around that time Abbott remembers hearing about what the pundits later dubbed, "Rick Santelli's Shout Heard 'Round the World." It was another spark lighting the engineer's political passion. The CNBC host has since been given some of the credit (or blame, depending on who you talk with), for igniting the Tea Party movement to some degree. In the depths of the market's meltdown, the angry Santelli blasted the bailouts with words that instantly became an internet sensation. It's something many people at the rallies, including Abbott, like to reference. "The government is promoting bad behavior," the business reporter said with his trademark intensity on televisions around the world. He continued:

> "You know, the new administration is big on computers and technology. How about this President and new administration? Why don't you put up a web site to have people

vote on the internet as a referendum to see if we really want to subsidize the losers' mortgages – or - would we like to at least buy cars and buy houses in foreclosure and give them to people that might have a chance to actually prosper down the road and reward people that can carry the water instead of drink the water?"

Traders in back of Santelli cheered.

"This is America," he said, staring right at the camera lens. "How many of you people want to pay for your neighbor's mortgage that has an extra bathroom and can't pay their bills? Raise their hand." (The traders booed at the thought). "President Obama are you listening? …Cuba used to have mansions and a relatively decent economy. They moved from the individual (to the) collective. Now they're driving '54 Chevy's, maybe the last great car to come out of Detroit…We're thinking of having a Chicago Tea Party in July. All you capitalists that want to show up to Lake Michigan – I'm going to start organizing…we're going to be dumping in some derivative securities.[1] You can't buy your way into prosperity. And if the

---

[1] The derivative securities Santelli spoke of are complicated investments that had spun out of control on Wall Street. They were the push that threatened to topple the financial dominoes. It's the subject of entire books, but basically – very basically - investment banks had turned mortgages into Wall Street investments. Those investments soon had little resemblance to the real homes that they were supposed to be based on and weren't as safe as the rating agencies said they were. Many people and institutions trust these agencies to tell them how risky an investment might be. With good ratings, more and more people around the globe bought up such ill-fated investments. All that needed to happen to bring the whole thing crashing down was for the houses underpinning the "derivatives" to go down in value. Especially because, at the same time, other investors figured out that those derivative investments weren't as solid as everyone thought. Those opportunists essentially bet against the housing market. They basically took out what amounted to insurance policies, so that if the investments did go bad, they could collect massive paydays. The problem with that side of the equation was that the companies selling the "insurance" investments didn't evaluate the risk properly, because, once again, the original investments weren't supposed to fail. So when it came to the so-called "insurance," devastating

multiplier that all of these Washington economists are selling us is over one, then we never have to worry about the economy again. The government should spend $1 trillion an hour, because we'll get $1.5 trillion back…I'll tell you what, if you read our Founding Fathers, people like Benjamin Franklin and Jefferson, what we're doing in this country is making them roll over in their graves."

After the rant, and after popular anger began spilling onto various media outlets across the nation, Abbott realized that he wasn't the only one thinking about organizing a rally. "None of us had done this before," he says. "I had never even attended one before." Unfortunately, Abbott also found out that you can't just hold a protest, especially if a few hundred people might actually show up. He hunted down the proper permits and moved the date back a bit as the Tea Party movement began to take shape around the country.

Abbott often spoke with a local radio DJ who was sympathetic to the Tea Party concerns, sometimes talking openly over the airwaves. They sent messages to each other and to their growing list of followers on Facebook. "So this is a brand new medium - social networking comes into play here," Abbott says. It was the "first time I had really been on Facebook or any of the social networking sites." It turned out that rallies were scheduled to take place on Tax Day, April 15th, in most major cities in the US. With some help from the Tea Party Express national co-founder, Amy Kremer, Abbott set up an e-mail account and became familiar with various web sites, "and the next thing you know I'm coordinating the Albany Tax Day Tea Party."

Abbott and a few other local organizers met as much as they could. He admits that at first he didn't think the movement was going anywhere. Ironically, or perhaps fittingly, they chose to meet at the local 76 Diner, something that they all now joke about. "I thought this was

---

mistakes were also being made by companies such as AIG. Like a game of musical chairs, the whole scheme worked as long as the investors believed houses could only increase in value. The music played on for several years. But once that music stopped, the money dried up and all the intertwined players of the financial system had to scramble to survive and find a seat. Not all of them did. (For a far better explanation of what happened, check out your local bookstore for books like "The Big Short: Inside the Doomsday Machine," by Michael Lewis.)

going to be a *get it off your chest* kind of thing," he says, "rail at the politicians, blow off some steam. And even at that time there was some rumblings at this becoming a movement. I joked with my wife, 'I can see it now, honey – the revolution began at the 76 Diner. What better a place for patriots?' But she would just roll her eyes. She would say, *Check your ego at the door, bud. Get over yourself.*"

Like a good husband, he makes sure to say that he's joking about that conversation with his wife. Although he admits his family may not feel as intensely as he does about politics, Abbott describes his wife as open-minded. "I think it would be easier for her to be supportive if we weren't struggling financially right now. I mean her focus is on – she's a great mother, great wife – it's - *make sure there's food on the table and a roof over our heads and the kids are growing up correctly.*" He toys with the idea of running for local office but isn't sure, especially with the sacrifice it would require from his family.

What the former Navy Supply Officer is sure about, though, is that he hates inefficiency. In Abbott's opinion, inefficiency wastes tax money and creates a host of other problems. And he's had enough. "The corruption," he says. "And we've seen it with both parties. Sure there's some good people out there, but not enough of them."

And he doesn't like how the government is wiggling into his life more and more. "The high taxes," he says, almost pleading for someone to do *something*. "And you combine the taxes and fees going up – but it seems stupid...I think it's another step towards the *nanny-state*. It's the intrusive government that bothers me so much. Yeah, I probably drink too much soda, but it's not your job to tell me that. It's my mother's job, it's my wife's job, it's my kid's job - it's *my* job ultimately. So quit taxing me for my health. Just back off." As a roller-coaster aficionado, Abbott says he was also irritated when Congressional leaders took it upon themselves to look at "G-Force limitations," basically, how much force a ride can exert on your body. He concedes that it's a matter of safety, but he just doesn't feel it was Congress' problem in the first place. "The more intrusive policies – that's what it boiled down to for the Tea Party. Intrusive government, higher taxes, out of control spending, corrupt career politicians, and an overall emphasis on the Constitution and Constitutional government."

Abbott worked behind the scenes on what became the April 15, 2009, Tea Party rally in Albany, New York. Estimates varied, but he thinks between two- and three-thousand people attended. A few months later they even put together another Tea Party gathering, trying to capitalize on the success of the first. There, the protestors carried all the usual signs and flags, although, the flags did look a little funny, or, at least, what they were tied to. For everybody's "safety," the protesters were forbidden from attaching their flags to the usual wooden poles. "The March on Albany we did in June - State Police said no flagpoles," Abbott explains. "No flags on flagpoles which just upset everybody. There were people saying, *I'm bringing my flag on a flagpole, and if they want to arrest me, they want to arrest me.* OK that's fine, if you want to risk that personally. But officially, I'm telling you that's not what we want. We're telling people not to do that. I want to work with the authorities - especially, the local police department. We work very well with them, and I don't want to do anything that will hurt that relationship. Quite frankly, I would bet a lot of the guys on the force themselves are supportive of the main messages being sent."

Still, Abbott's biggest concern as an organizer is something that Tea Party critics have also talked about. "I'm almost reticent to say it," he says, pausing to think. "Violence is a big fear of mine. There are a lot of people who are really upset out there. I'm one for peaceful reform. I think it needs to be peaceful. I'd say back in the 1700's the Revolutionary War, while not the ideal situation, was the only way freedom was going to come to the Colonists. I don't think that's the situation we're in right now. "My fear is you get a couple of crazies out there – and we've already seen a couple...not that I'd call him a Tea Partier by any stretch, but the guy who crashed his plane into the IRS building." The thought forces him to think deeply about the implications. He now asks himself, "If we get a few more of those, will there be a government attempt – by government, I mean leadership, President, members of Congress - to link the Tea Party to other violent groups? If that ever happens, that's not a good thing for the country and not a good thing for the movement."

Because as much as Abbott wants to stir the political pot, he doesn't seem to want it to boil over. "I have concerns if the argument goes too far one way or the other in the Tea Party movement," he says.

But sometimes the arguments do stray from the mainstream path, and it begs for a number of questions to be asked. After all, rarely is there a Tea Party rally without someone questioning if President Obama was actually born in the United States. And if you didn't run into a so-called *birther*, perhaps you would meet someone who would passionately tell you that the Federal Reserve, which sets monetary policy and interest rates in the US, was really an evil group of bankers bent on taking over the world. Or, maybe you would hear from a so-called *truther*, arguing that 9/11 was "an inside job" and that there's all this data from engineers to support their claim. "There are some fringe folks on there, and I'm not even sure – let me be clear – I wouldn't necessarily put some *End the Fed* folks in that," Abbott says. "But the *birthers* and *truthers*. You know, I'm not a conspiracy guy. It's kind of fun to do it. I enjoyed watching the *X-Files*, things like that when it was on. But I'm not out there – I tend to believe the government does not have the capability to keep a secret well enough in most cases. I suppose it's possible. Even in the military, which I thought was *relatively* efficient - I just don't see that capability. Now, I could be wrong."

When it comes to where President Obama was born, Abbott stops short of admitting he believes the *birther's* arguments, but he doesn't sound sure that the President is a US citizen, either. Still, the Obama administration had released documents showing he was born in Hawaii. A number of mainstream media outlets had reported on those documents, though that doesn't mean it holds water with everyone in the Tea Party movement. Regardless, to Abbott, it's beside the point. "What's that going to accomplish right now?" he asks. "Even if it turns out he's legally, constitutionally the president but not born in the US, whatever - is that going to change the fact we're already two years into his Presidency? It's a little late for that now. All I think that's going to do is precipitate a Constitutional crisis. We don't need that. And quite frankly, I don't think we need to get Nancy Pelosi any closer to the Presidency than we already have."

Abbott says he has looked into some of the claims from *truthers* about 9/11 too. Admittedly, it's a tough, emotional topic. For some people, even suggesting the conspiracy theory is utterly offensive, almost treasonous. Others argue that asking such questions is the duty of free people. But if you can get past the initial gut reaction, at least to some degree, then you will inevitably hear from some that 9/11 wasn't an attack by Al Qaida operatives, but instead, was an *inside job*. They'll tell you that one of the buildings that housed top government agencies near the Twin Towers collapsed, almost as if in free-fall, although it was never hit by any planes. And some then argue that if the whole attack was contrived, it was done to take people's civil liberties away under the guise of safety. For his part, Abbott doesn't buy it, although, there are those who do. "They're just – come on," Abbott says, looking for the right words. "I watched it on TV myself. And I've got enough engineering background to know that when an airplane flies into a building, there's reasonable reason for that building to come down. I've read through some of the reports from one of the government agencies that investigated the collapse – even down to some of the engineering reasons as to why the metal softened and things like that. I have a materials engineering background so there was enough in there that it made sense to me. No, I'm not one of those conspiracy nuts," he continues. "Do they exist on the fringe of the Tea Party? Not any more so than they exist on the fringe of the Democrat or Republican party or Libertarian party…There's still a core group that's focused on the main part. I think the fringe folks exist everywhere. And quite frankly, I think they're a little more fun."

Of course, the theories about how the world might really function don't stop there. Just visit a Tea Party rally and you'll find you can purchase books on everything from Thomas Jefferson to the New World Order. Jefferson might be self-explanatory, but if the New World Order is something you don't ever remember hearing about, here's an oversimplification of the theory: a world government will eventually take shape by design, and it will supposedly be controlled by the world's elite to further enrich themselves and gain ultimate power. Incrementally, the story goes, they are building their new world, and they're doing it just slowly enough so that no one wakes up. It's sort of like the tale we've all heard about involving the pot sitting on a stove, a pot filled with a little bit of water and a frog inside. The frog never notices that he's being boiled as long as the burner only *gradually* gets hotter. According to the political theory, ever so slowly, the elite are gaining control of every aspect of our lives, taking advantage of world crises to tighten their grip. For instance, some say *they* are destroying the dollar *on purpose* in order to move the United States to a regional currency shared by Canada and Mexico, dubbed *the Amero*, before creating an international currency giving them total control. It's actually a pretty complicated theory of the world, true or not.

"That's an area where years ago I have to admit I would have ignored (it) and said it's not worth looking at," Abbott says. Again, he is choosing his words carefully, trying to make sure he conveys his thoughts clearly. He doesn't want to come off as one of the protestors who's on the fringe of the movement, but he doesn't want to dodge my questions, either. "The Federal Reserve – I just realize from my own research that I don't know enough about it. It's kind of murky, a little bit. I would go as far as to say we need to audit the Fed. I'm not sure ending the Fed is the way to go. I just don't have enough personal knowledge. The more openness we can show the better."

But what about the *one-world government* theory? "I've been starting to read up on the crisis over in Europe with the Euro and Greece playing into the mix. I could see how some of that spooky one-world currency stuff gets...." His voice trails off as he ponders how to explain what he's thinking as he tries to answer these tough questions. "A couple of decades ago, would you have really thought there would be a single European currency? No. No hope for that whatsoever." After all, "back when I was in the Navy, I was a dispersing officer. I wouldn't have even dreamed of a single European currency at that time. I know they were talking about it, but at that time I was handling the ship's cash. I saw all sorts of currency pass through. And quite frankly, some of me would miss some of that."

He jokes that the Euro would have made things far easier, at least after one night of drinking in Spain with a friend. "Catching a cab, (my friend) handed me all of his money which was in at least four or five currencies and said, 'Hey, pay the cab driver.' I have no idea. We may have paid that cab driver $1,000 or more. We had Italian Lira and (Greek) Drachma. It would have been a lot easier if we had the Euro at the time. But yeah, there needs to be some light shed on that. But at the same time I'm not ready to say there's a New World Order conspiracy out there. Could there be? Anything's possible."

Theories of world government aside, Abbott seems far more focused on the local impact of the Tea Parties. It's what he prefers to talk about. His biggest hope isn't one that he thinks most Tea Partiers would approve of. "If you ask other people, it might be getting a Tea Partier elected President or something like that," he says. "I don't think it's that. For me, maybe I'm not dreaming big enough, but my biggest hope would be on the local level to have this organization play an important role. Yeah, get someone elected. Get a good citizen legislator - or legislators - elected. I don't think it would take much. People who say, *throw all the bums out* – I don't think you necessarily have to." Abbott thinks that just a few Tea Partiers in key locations could tip the balance and put some of the current politicians on notice that the people are watching. Such Tea Politicians could drive politics not more *left* or *right*, he says, "but away from corruption. Idealistic? Probably. But it would be nice to have."

Meanwhile, as most people involved with the Tea Party seem to advocate fiscally conservative ideals, a return to a strict interpretation of the Constitution, and pure political motives, that purity is getting challenged as the movement grows. "Not so much corporate," Abbott says, "but certainly political influence. I've got friend requests, calls, e-mails (from) people running for office, some of which I've never heard of before, some of which are a little *fringier* than my tastes." But, he says that mainstream politicians, especially Republicans, have only really "put out feelers" trying to court the Tea Party. At the same time, he makes it clear that he hasn't seen anything over-the-top. "I haven't seen a lot of pressure, or even the typical *you pat my back, I'll pat your back,* sort of thing. Right now I'd say it's more about building relationships. Could it turn that way down the road? Nationally, maybe. But not here."

Abbott says he doesn't put a lot of stock into "Constitutional Conventions," at least for now. He's not sure if the movement will become a legitimate political party, a regular staple of the voting booth. "There is a big Libertarian influence," he says. "There's also a lot of Republicans. We've seen some Democrats too. Not huge numbers, but we've seen some there. We've seen - I'd say the best way to describe it is fiscally conservative, Constitutional-type government. There are certainly differences of opinion. On the core issues I just talked about, there's relative agreement. But you look at any of the major parties, there's disagreement on how to do specifics. The Tea Party is no different."

He clarifies that he's not insinuating the Tea Party will become an organized party like the Democrats and Republicans because he thinks it's just too early to know. "From day one the argument has been – do you reform government from the inside, i.e. most likely the Republican party? Though, there has also been talk about doing the same through the Democratic Party. I mean there are good Democrats out there. A couple at least. A couple of them," he jokes. Abbott believes that bottom line, the strength and longevity of the Tea Party hinges on successfully answering the question of whether to become a third party, or whether they should work from *within* the current parties. He thinks it won't be easy because he believes the question should be answered on a case-by-case basis. "I think there are times it's appropriate to start a third party," he says. Yet, in his own town a number of Tea Party candidates ran in a recent election - and they all lost. "It gave Democrats the control of pretty much the entire town. And while that may bother some, like the hard-line Republicans, on the local level, Democrat versus Republican, doesn't matter to me as much as the person and what they're talking about. I mean filling potholes, a Democrat can do that as well as a Republican as well as an Independent."

Still, others might say the local Tea Party candidates had split the vote, in other words, that they'd rather see conservative Republicans lose to more liberal Democrats, if it means a Tea Partier gets to make a point. "There was that aspect and that argument was made," Abbott says. "On the other hand, it may have been the right thing to do. And the percentages that these guys got they shouldn't have gotten. You're talking one of the (Tea Party) candidates got 20% of the vote." He argues it was the right thing to do "because it's a longer-term issue. It's more than the ends justifying the means. If you want to shake up politics, you have to look at those situations."

The more Abbott involves himself in politics, the more he comes to believe that the system only survives when people are actively engaged. "I used to think it was enough to sit on the sidelines and vote and that was doing my duty," he says. "And I think for a lot of people that may still be the case. What I found is it really doesn't take that many people to change it. Here I am. You know, by all rights, I should not be a player at all at any level in the local or national or statewide political movement. I don't want to sound egotistical here. It's not as if I didn't come in, this movement wouldn't have come into fruition. It would have. I'm just one player. I think that's what's important. I think an *Average Joe* - or the term I've come up with is *Ordinary Citizen* - can make a huge difference just by stepping up. And it may not take a lot. Maybe you go find the right person and go walk door-to-door for him. Maybe you get on the phone for him, go on the campaign. Maybe *you're* that right person. A lot of ordinary people have stepped up and run for office that would not have done that."

Abbott says he brings his two children to the rallies and will continue doing so as long as they all feel safe. So far, he's had no cause for concern. Abbott says that instead, attending the events has been educational for both him and his children. Additionally, he now takes every chance to urge people to do more than just vote. And he still has faith in the system and hope for his children's future. "I intend to show them what it means to be a patriot. I want to talk to them about my military experience, give them a good feel for history in the US."

Abbott's two-year-old is far too young to understand any of it, but when his four-year-old gets in the car, he now asks, "are we going to a Tea Party, dad?" Abbott laughs: "So I have a feeling he's going to grow up not understanding, you know, when the little girls talk about having a tea party, he's going to view it as a protest with a bunch of signs."

Chapter VII

The Presidential Candidate

"There's a part of the Tea Party movement that actually did exist before I was elected. We saw some of it leading up to my election. There were some folks who just weren't sure whether I was born in the United States, whether I was a socialist.

"I think that there's a broader circle around that core group of people who are legitimately concerned about the deficit, who are legitimately concerned that the federal government may be taking on too much.

"And so I wouldn't paint in a broad brush and say that everybody who is involved or have gone to a Tea Party rally or meeting are somehow on the fringe. Some of them, I think, have some legitimate, mainstream concerns. And my hope is that as we move forward and we're tackling things like the deficit, imposing a freeze on domestic spending, taking steps that show we are sincere about dealing with our long-term problems - that some of that group will dissipate."

-President Barack Obama

March 30, 2010

Interview on "The Today Show"

     Michael Badnarik worries that the United States of America is in free-fall. Speaking with an intellectual ferocity not common to American conversation, it's as if each word he utters is calculated to leave an impression. And yet, while his name might be familiar to some, others who haven't followed the latest political news might have to take a minute to remember who he is. For most, it would probably bring them back to the voting booth; his name was listed on the ballot across the country for President. But, of course, he'll tell you that his walk down the path that now converges in many ways with the Tea Party began long before the movement became *the* big political topic. "Where's everybody been all this time?" he wonders aloud from his Texas home. "I started studying the Constitution 28 years ago and came to a rapid conclusion that most of what our government does is unconstitutional."

     With salt-and-pepper hair, eyes that indicate his brain is firing on all cylinders, and a clear control over American history, Badnarik says he never thought he would end up *here* politically - a libertarian philosophy couched in concern for America, and all of it based on the Constitution. He says that it took him some time to accept his interpretation of the Constitution because it revealed to him a government that barely resembles the one that the Founders created. "My first reaction was denial. I couldn't actually believe that was true," he says incredulously. "However, further study, further research, convinced me that it was, in fact, true. Someone recommended that I read a book called, *The Creature from Jekyll Island*, written by my good friend, G. Edward Griffin. And that book is what got me into this crusade for liberty. And it wasn't because the book convinced me I was wrong. The book convinced me it was much worse than I had thought."

It wasn't only the book that brought him to this intellectual viewpoint. It also took a calculator. Badnarik says, "In the mid-eighties I was living and working in California. I had an excellent job. I was a high-priced computer programmer and a technical trainer and was traveling around California quite a bit. Being a bachelor, I would cash my check, pay the bills, and really not worry about a budget. But I realized that even with the amount of money I was making, I never had a lot of money left over. You know, after you pay the rent and the car insurance and the cable television, there wasn't much money left to go visit a party. So I decided it was time for me to create a spreadsheet and really establish a budget. Well, the first thing I did was to create a spreadsheet and record the federal, state, and FICA taxes that were being deducted. And I quickly realized that my federal statement and FICA taxes totaled 48 percent. Now, I don't know where you went to school, but when I was going to school, 48 percent was half. The government was taking half of everything I made. I didn't know very much about the IRS at the time, but even if the IRS were a legitimate organization, I knew that I was not going to give *half* of my bodily effort to the government. I wasn't. I made a decision at that point in time - if the government wanted more than half, they were going to have to come with a shotgun and take it."

Badnarik speaks with continuous intensity, as if trying to goad me into asking if he is serious. There is no need to ask him, though. His tone is clearly nothing but serious. "I would go around and, naturally, when you're irritated about something, you converse with people about it," he says. "I would talk with people about the state of affairs…and people would make statements that Social Security is in the Constitution. And I would know that to not be true. And I would hand them a copy of the Constitution and say, 'Show me. Show me where in the Constitution you can find Social Security.' Well, naturally, they couldn't find it. This kind of thing happened so often that I realized people have no idea what the Constitution says."

At that time, Badnarik says the idea jumped out at him to put together a series of twelve video lessons about the Constitution. However, fitting all that he wanted to say into a dozen videos was too daunting a task. "As I sat down to create the script for this video, I realized three hours would never be enough," he explains. "Eventually, I created an eight-hour class on the Constitution. Originally, I only charged two ounces of silver at the time, which at the time was $20."

Badnarik doesn't say it, but sometimes, when an idea resonates with others, it has a way of taking off in ways never imagined. While the internet was certainly coming into many households at the time – which happened to be the week before the attacks of September 11th - most people probably weren't too knowledgeable with uploading videos. YouTube hadn't even been invented yet. But during that week in 2001, a student videotaped Badnarik's class. Soon after, the student informed him that it was quickly spreading across the internet. "Now my Constitution class is available on some 350 websites," says Badnarik. "I don't know if there's any way to estimate how many people have viewed my class, but many of those sites have had 50,000 viewings just on one site. So if you just extrapolate that out, there are probably one million to two million people who have watched my Constitution class. *That* is spreading the word. I am certainly not arrogant enough to believe that my Constitution class has caused the Tea Party movement, but I will suspect that many of the people in the Tea Party movement have seen my class."

Badnarik has taught the class ever since, catching planes at odd hours to cities all over the country. In between, he even found time to run for national office. He ran for Congress in 2005 and in 2006 - in addition to an earlier campaign for president - all the while spreading the libertarian word. "The thing that surprises me most of all is how little people really know about the Constitution," Badnarik says one more time to drive home the point. "I will frequently give a presentation to an auditorium and my first request is, 'Raise your hand if you're a good, patriotic American.' And naturally everyone raises their hands. Everybody considers themselves a good, patriotic American. And the next request or question is, 'Please raise your hand if you can tell me how many articles are in the Constitution.' Sadly, rarely does anybody raise their hand. Well, what is the standard for being a good, patriotic American - you know how to get dressed by yourself? That's the standard we set? I think we need to set that standard much higher.

"I can teach people the difference between rights and privileges. I can remind them that *we, the people*, are the source of all political power in the United States. You know, the Declaration of Independence says we can alter or abolish the government. That's a lot of power. And the Tea Party movement, though I consider it to be very late in coming, is a manifestation of the fact that people are tired of the status quo. They are tired of voting for the lesser of two evils. The economy is so bad that even having two parents working, frequently does not pay the rent or put food on the table. People are now living on credit card debt. They are using their credit card to purchase food for the family, just to survive. And much of my early political career people said, 'Well, people don't get involved unless they feel it in their pocketbook.' And I believe that the Tea Party rally is evidence that everybody is feeling it in their pocketbook."

But what if there really is an economic recovery happening? Would the Tea Parties simply dissipate, like the proverbial tempest in a teapot? "I do believe that more and more people are waking up," he starts to explain. "Because even though the American people don't know the Constitution - they don't know the Bill of Rights like they should - they *do* know that there's an economic recovery that falls in the same category as *the check is in the mail*, and, *of course I'll respect you in the morning*. Of course they know that that's a lie.

"We have, I'm guessing, somewhere in the neighborhood of 18-20 percent unemployment. You know, the mainstream media is reporting twelve percent." However, the problem isn't the unemployment statistics, or even how they're reported, he says. In his opinion, it's a *systemic* failure. "It's not possible for the economy to recover without it getting much worse. The Federal Reserve has printed so much money recently that there is an economic tidal wave headed in our direction. If you think that money is worthless right now, wait until it becomes worth *less*."

Badnarik continues with a lesson in history that many Americans probably haven't heard much about. "There's several examples," he says. "The money in Mexico. Mexico has been printing money so fast that if you see a peso on the ground, you won't pick it up. I mean it's not worth the effort to bend over, whereas if you see a washer on the ground, you might actually pick that up because a washer can actually be used for something."

I asked him if he was getting at the idea shared by many in the Tea Party that valuable metals should be used as money. Just ask, and a good portion of the protestors will likely tell you that they believe that the economy can't ever truly be free unless gold and silver are used in trade, instead of paper and valueless coins that the government tells people to use – by law. "Well, we do have an answer for this," Badnarik begins, sounding surprised that more people haven't heard of such ideas. Or perhaps, he's a little ticked that most people haven't bothered to investigate what at first would seem to be a rather dry subject. "First of all, those people who fail to study history are doomed to repeat it. Unfortunately, history has shown that people never study history. I read a quote recently that says there is no present, there is no future. There is only the past happening over and over and over again."

He returns to a discussion of Mexico. "It was many years ago. I remember when Mexico just arbitrarily deleted three zeroes off the end of their money. They just devalued it by a thousand. And most people remember the story about Weimar Republic in Germany. After the first World War, Germany was required to pay back incredible war reparations - millions or billions of dollars in war reparations. But the Treaty of Versailles forbid them to do any manufacturing, anything that would actually create wealth. And the only option left to the German government was to print money, and they went into that with a vengeance. They were printing money so fast that prices would increase at the store several times a day. There would be a morning price, an afternoon price, an evening price. When workers would get paid, they would rush to the fence and hand the money to their wives who would then spend the money – all of the money that afternoon - before the money became devalued more than it was."

Is that where he honestly believes the United States is headed? It is, after all, a major accusation since it had taken *major* events to create the Weimar Republic's financial mess. "Oh, absolutely," Badnarik answers, as if he's shocked that anyone would think America *wasn't* destined for financial ruin. "Absolutely. In 1913, Congress unconstitutionally and treasonously passed the Federal Reserve Act." Without skipping a beat, he recites from memory that, "Article I Section 8 Clause 5 of the Constitution gives Congress the power to coin money and regulate the value thereof. It explicitly does not give them the power to print money. And you can verify that by reading the Federalist Papers and James

Madison's notes on the Constitutional Convention. *Congress* is allowed to coin money. Congress is *not allowed* to give that authority to someone else. If I'm a police officer, I can't hand you my pistol and ask you to write traffic tickets for me. That's my responsibility…Congress cannot give away its responsibility - and Congress never had the authority to *print* money. So how can Congress give the Federal Reserve, which is a private organization, the power to print money when Congress didn't have that authority themselves? It would be like handing you an apple I don't have. If I don't have an apple, how can I give you one? The Federal Reserve Act of 1913 is blatantly, totally, 100 percent unconstitutional, and if there're any members of Congress still alive (who voted for it), they should be arrested and put in jail for life for treason."

Of course, Badnarik is just getting started. He says he feels there has been a major shift in how many Americans view politics. For instance, over the last several decades, debates have largely been between people adamant about one issue - pro-choice versus pro-life, or gun control versus gun rights, for example. But the Tea Party movement is one where people speak about multiple issues. They see the very same government in a very different light. "Well, this is the Second American Revolution," Badnarik says. "Benjamin Franklin defined *revolution* as an astronomical term. When the Earth revolves around the sun, it comes back to its original starting point." He believes that the hearts and minds of Americans are approaching a similar situation hundreds of years later. "When Benjamin Franklin analyzed history, he would acknowledge that we all started out as hunters and gatherers with private property. We didn't have much private property, but it was ours. And somehow humans got away from the idea of private property and devolved into something known as the Divine Right of Kings where the king or the emperor owned everything. King George owned all of England (and) the thirteen colonies. He owned large territories around the world, even though he had never physically been there. In 1760 in the Colonies, if you asked someone, 'Who owned the Colonies?' the incredulous answer would be, 'Well, King George III, of course.' Fifteen years later in 1775, people in the Colonies were none too happy with the king. And so this is what Benjamin Franklin defines as the real American Revolution. It was a change in the way the people think. At one point they like the king, and much later they decided the king is not such a great idea. We are in the Second American Revolution right now using that definition. People are changing the way they think.

"Back in 1933 during the Great Depression, everybody assumed the federal government should be in charge because the federal government will take care of everything. They'll take care of your retirement, they'll take care of your children's education. They'll take care of health care. And over the last two years I would say, people have begun to realize that the government doesn't take care of very much. When we examine the end result of Hurricane Katrina and the disaster in New Orleans, the federal government was miserable in taking care of things…They refused to allow people out of New Orleans, people who were trying to escape the city. And, as far as I'm concerned, the worst part was sending in the National Guard to go door-to-door confiscating people's guns."

So where do all these Tea Party protests lead America? Like others in the movement, he believes that the faster people open up to Tea Party ideals, the better the possibility of a *peaceful* outcome. "It is a prelude, but it's not preordained. This is not fate. We don't have to sit here and let all these bad things happen. Benjamin Franklin says a revolution is a change in the way people think, and in 1775 we started a bloody rebellion to defend the ideas, defend the way that we think. Benjamin Franklin indicated that if you have the revolution early enough and you change the way people think quickly enough, then it is possible to avoid or mitigate the bloody rebellion.

"Given that things have changed so dramatically in the last two years, I am hopeful that the American people will wake up, that the Tea Party members will become educated. Because the members of the Tea Party at this point are angry - they're angry with the government. However, knowing what you don't like is not the same as knowing what you do like." Badnarik uses this analogy: "You know, if you are lost in the forest, I think you're pretty clear if you don't like being in the forest where you are. But if you don't know how to get home, you are still lost in the forest. And politically, over the last 50 to 100 years, people have been lost in the political forest. You know, they get lost in the Democratic area of the forest, and then they rush to the Republican area of the forest. When they can't find a home there, they rush back to the Democratic area of the forest. And we're basically traveling in circles and we are still lost. What people need in order to find their way to liberty, they need to follow their Constitutional compass. They need to know which direction liberty is in. They need to know what liberty is and how to get it. Once they understand the Constitution – if they understand the

Constitution – then, and only then, will they be able to travel in a straight line from the tyranny that we have to the liberty that they want."

It is intense talk, but it does seem to match many of the arguments emanating from Tea Party voices all over the country. And it was a very similar message that Badnarik brought to a national audience when he ran for President in 2004. He says he had no intention of running for the office – not even a thought. At the time he was teaching his Constitution classes. True, he had run a campaign for Texas State Representative, but he admits that it "was simply a vehicle for me to get in front of a microphone and reach more people."

Then, Badnarik was invited to give the warm-up speech in San Antonio for another political candidate. He accepted the offer and spoke about the Constitution, Liberty, Freedom, and the Founding Fathers. "And I got a standing ovation," he recalls. "I was flattered, and the only thing I suspected was that my rhetoric was becoming a little bit more polished. Well, a day or so later on my way to work, a friend called me on the phone and said, 'We want you to run for President.' I said, 'President of what?' He said, 'President of the United States.' I said, 'You've got to be kidding.' I was living at the poverty level and you go from the poor house to the White House? That's ridiculous."

The conversation would change his life. It took some convincing, but eventually he decided to jump in. Badnarik realized the odds of winning would be slim, but he also viewed it as another chance to spread the word. "And much to my surprise, in May of 2004 at the Libertarian National Convention in Atlanta, I won the debate. The following day I won the nomination." Thus began his long-shot bid to become the next president of the United States.

During that campaign season, millions of Americans watched the televised debate between President George W. Bush and Senator John Kerry in 2004 at Washington University in St. Louis, Missouri. Charlie Gibson of ABC News moderated the town hall-style forum. One-hundred-and-forty "undecided voters" asked questions of the two candidates. The major issue that night was the Iraq War, and Senator Kerry tried to convince voters he wasn't a *flip-flopper* on his political beliefs; President Bush tried to convince people that Kerry was. Most Americans probably never even realized that outside the debate venue, two other candidates vying for the most powerful office in the world were being placed in the back of a police van.

"I was arrested in St. Louis, Missouri, along with my good friend, David Cobb, who was the Green Party candidate in 2004," Badnarik says. "David invited me to engage in civil disobedience with him. The only thing I disagree with is the definition of civil disobedience. I have freedom of speech, and so given the fact that David and I were legitimate presidential candidates attempting to attend the presidential debate is not civil disobedience. The civil disobedience happened when David and I were arrested, handcuffed, and put into a police van. And as David and I sat there in our jackets and ties and handcuffs, about 20 minutes later a police officer opened the doors to the van and said, 'Which of you is a presidential candidate?' And I looked at the police officer and I said, 'We are both presidential candidates. We are at a presidential debate. If you have us in handcuffs,' I said, 'Can *you* explain that to *me?*' And the police officer said, 'Let me get back to you on that.'"

Badnarik figured at the time that both he and Cobb would be hauled off to jail and probably fined. Before that happened, though, the police van that had begun to transport them wherever they were headed to, abruptly stopped. "After another ten minutes, the doors open and they throw five college students into the back of the van. All the students are handcuffed. Now these college students, even if they were vaguely aware there was a presidential debate on campus, they were probably some of the more enlightened students," he jokes. The students told him that "on their way home from class (they) decided to take a shortcut through a meadow. There was no police ribbon, there were no barricades. There was no indication the meadow was off-limits because the President was in town. As the students walked across the meadow, suddenly, people in black ski masks and black ninja outfits jumped out of nowhere and threw them to the ground. And the students thought they were going to die. This is America...the students later said they were thrilled to discover they were only being arrested. Given a choice between being murdered in the dark and being arrested, it is *far* better. And so these college students are escorted into the van. They're looking at two adult males in jackets and ties, handcuffed in the back of a police van.

"Now if you thought that David and I were confused, I mean we knew why we were there, but the expressions on the faces of these college kids was priceless. They said, 'Well, who are you?' And I said, 'My name is Michael Badnarik, and I'm running for president of the United States.' And they go, 'Yeah buddy, sure you are.' And I go, 'No, this is David Cobb, he's the candidate of the Green party, and I'm the presidential candidate for the Libertarian party. And there's a presidential debate that we wanted to attend, and we got arrested because the mainstream media, the Democrats and Republicans, don't want us on the stage. They don't want us mentioning the Constitution.'"

As Badnarik tells it, "When the students realized that we were telling the truth, they were excited. They could not believe their good fortune to be arrested and put in the same police van with two presidential candidates…they couldn't wait to get out of jail and tell all their friends." The whole ordeal might be laughable if Badnarik wasn't so concerned that his rights as a citizen and as a presidential candidate had been denied.

Of course, the US electorate didn't elect a president by the name of Michael Badnarik. But his journey through the political process left him with this belief: "After running for President, and then running for Congress in 2005 and 2006, I have come to the conclusion that if voting in the United States made a difference, it would be illegal. We have electronic voting machines in nearly every precinct in the United States. Being a computer programmer for nearly 40 years, if you allow me to write the software and keep that software proprietary, I will tell you who is going to win by exactly what percentage margin before the polls even open. *What would you like the results to be?*"

It's certainly not a new theory, and anyone with a little time on their hands can look up a number of videos on the internet to find entire debates and discussions on the topic. Those whose job it is to protect the sanctity of the election system in America will vehemently deny that electronic voting fraud has happened, is happening, or is even possible. So, again, this was a major accusation. "It is an incredible accusation, and they've been analyzing this – voter fraud – for the last 20, 25 years," he says. He gives an example of the TV remote control to show how it could be done. "You know, you push the button and you change the channel. Push the button, change the volume. All of those things happen *automagically*. Well, it's not magic. It's an infrared coded signal. If you look at the tip of your remote control there's usually a little glass bead which is like a flashlight. And you're shining this invisible light at the VCR or the television, and it's sending a little Morse Code signal that the volume should go up, the channel should go down…All of these different signals are coded and transmitted to the device. Well, if you can change the channel and the volume on your television, you can use a little remote control device to walk by the voting machine, and after a whole day of voting, the voting machine may contain an accurate vote of whom voted for whom. And in 30 to 45 seconds, you can change the result of the votes."

That such a thing could specifically happen to voting machines has never been documented. Even if such a remote control exists, no voting machine with a receiver capable of changing the vote has ever been discovered. But true or not, the mere *possibility* seems to be the problem for Badnarik. So what does he suggest America should do about it? Once more, he returns to history's example. "In 1774, the members of the Colonies were upset with taxes. They were upset with many of the laws the king had imposed on them. They were upset they had very little control over their local legislation. And most of all, they were upset that the king was unwilling to negotiate. The king was not willing to listen to their complaints. If you're familiar with the Declaration of Independence, you'll know that it says, 'Our repeated petitions have been answered only by repeated injury.' And any king that has all these traits is a tyrant. So the result is they had run out of options. So they gathered people together – representatives and delegates from each of the 13 Colonies - and they sent the delegates to Philadelphia to analyze the situation. You know, talk it over and give us a recommendation as to what you would do next. The recommendation they eventually made is called the Declaration of Independence, where the 13 Colonies declared themselves to be free, sovereign, and independent states.

"We are in the same political position the Colonies were in, in 1774. We have tried voting. That doesn't work. We've tried calling our representatives. That doesn't work. We've tried writing nasty letters to the editor. That doesn't work. And even when we gather at the Capitol and hold protest rallies, that doesn't work because they send out the riot police and they beat people with their nightsticks - you know - they spray us with their tear gas and mace. So as much as we attempt to change the political structure legitimately and peacefully, all of our petitions have been answered only by repeated injury. So in November of 2009, from November 11 to November 22, delegates from 48 states gathered in St. Charles, Illinois, for Continental Congress 2009."

Most Americans have probably never heard about a 2009 Continental Congress, I tell Badnarik. "Unfortunately not," he replies. "Unfortunately, the mainstream media basically ignored it, but the same thing was true in 1774. Most people knew there was a problem, but most people really didn't know that a group of delegates had gotten together to analyze the situation and to advocate for their rights and their liberty. So this is the same result that we had in 1774. Delegates got together. They analyzed the situation," he says. Badnarik himself was a Texas delegate to the 2009 convention. Once he and the other delegates arrived in St. Charles from all over the country, they nominated him as the President of the Congress. He says each and every one of them worked long hours, sometimes fighting sleep until three or four in the morning, waking only a few hours later to continue their work.

"We analyzed what the Constitution said, we analyzed what the government was doing, and how that explicitly violated the Constitution. And we offered remedial instructions to the federal government, and we offered remedial instructions to the state governments. We are explicitly (arguing) in writing – *this is what you are doing wrong* – *and this is how we want you to fix it.* We are not asking, we are telling. We are the source of all political power in the United States, and right now, we are attempting to alter the government of the United States. And the implicit threat is, if the Articles of Freedom do not rally the people, if the members of our federal and state legislatures do not respond, then the people of the United States may be required to abolish this form of government and to start all over. We've done that once in history. We began with the Articles of Confederation, and we decided those did not suffice, and we threw the Articles of Confederation in the garbage can and came up with the Constitution in order to form *a more perfect union* - more perfect than the Articles of Confederation which we started with. So the Constitution is not a perfect document. But even if it was, even admitting for the moment that it was a perfect document, if nobody reads the Constitution and nobody understands the ideas written there, and if people do not stand up to defend those principles, then the Constitution is worthless. At that point you may as well burn the Constitution. You may as well shred the Bill of Rights. You may as well just give up and walk into the concentration camps and admit that you're a slave. Well, I know not what course others may take, but as for me, *give me liberty, or give me death.* I will not submit to a tyrannical government. I will not sit down when they tell me that this is not a free speech zone. I will not hand over my guns when they insist that I must be disarmed."

We both take a breath as we shift topics. I ask him if the heart attack he suffered just days before Christmas in 2009 forced him to think about his life and accomplishments. Badnarik says he doesn't remember most of the ordeal. According to reports, he slumped over during a trip to Wisconsin. His friends attempted to revive him using CPR, needing three tries to succeed. "When I regained consciousness," he says, "the hospital had a counselor come into my room, and the woman and I eventually became very good friends. But her statement to me was, 'You realize you've been given a second chance.' She was there to rattle my cage and get me to analyze my life, basically your question. My response to her was, well, 'You've been given a second chance too.' And she was startled: 'I haven't had a heart attack.' And I said, 'No, but you did wake up this morning, and that was not a guarantee. Just because you haven't experienced a heart attack yet doesn't mean your body isn't ready to shut down and have you die in your sleep.'"

He began to tell the counselor a little about his life. "I explained to her, as a skydiving instructor, I was far more conscious of death than most people." Badnarik says he has jumped out of planes more than 1,500 times. "Because every person who jumps out of a perfectly good airplane realizes that if they don't pull the ripcord, they are going to die. Skydivers don't jump out of planes because they have a death wish. They jump out of planes because they have a life wish. We know that life is finite. We know that everybody is going to die. And we know that your life is only as valuable as you make it while you're alive.

"I understand life better than most of the people in the hospital," he says. "I've been mountain climbing and sailing and skydiving and SCUBA diving and camping. My parents took my brothers and I to 48 of the continental United States. I have run for president. I've run for Congress. I teach a class. I am doing everything I possibly can to make my life valuable *now*. If you're laying in the hospital and the doctors have given you a week or so to live, it's too late to decide you're going to do something with your life. At that point where the doctors have given you a week to live, the only thing you have an opportunity to do is to live the flashbacks and go over the memories and analyze your life. And I am too terrified to think that I'm laying there in bed going, *you know, I've had this opportunity and I didn't take it.*

"Well, we have an unfortunate opportunity. The Founding Fathers helped us establish liberty back in the 1700's, and over the course of the last 234 years, we, the people, have allowed liberty and freedom to slip through our fingers. You know, this is a time for all of the summer soldiers and sunshine patriots to get up off the couch, turn off the television, and stand up in defense of liberty. Because, if we don't defend liberty, if we don't restore liberty and we don't do it right now, we may lose it forever."

America's economic free-fall may have ignited the Tea Party. But, like Badnarik's skydiving experiences, a free-fall doesn't have to mean the end. As he sees it, Tea Party ideals might just provide the opportunity for a better life in the midst of the challenges and controversies facing the United States of America.

Maybe that's the feeling that almost anyone at a Tea Party rally would try to convey to you as you talk. Whether it's the Gold-Star Mom who fights for a return to the ideals of the Founding Fathers, the attorney whose libertarian voice is increasingly getting heard, the sheriff who keeps the Constitution close to his heart, the entrepreneur who prefers the possibility of success to a costly social safety net, the elderly couple that fears America is on an unhealthy, unsustainable path, the Tea Party organizer who hopes the movement continues to challenge the status quo, or the presidential candidate who wishes people would seize today's "unfortunate opportunity" to use their "Constitutional compass," these are just some of their hopes and fears. They are the intimate thoughts and ideas that are rumbling across the countryside like a coming storm. It may only be the beginning of the conversation, but it's a dialogue that average folks are having over dinner in homes from New York to California. They are voices in search of justice for today's *forgotten Americans*, the people who are tired of being taken for granted by a political system that they feel is no longer working for them. The question now is this: will the rest of America begin to see their country in the way that the folks at the Tea Parties do? The answer to that question may very much define the future of the most powerful country in the world.

In Congress, July 4, 1776

The Unanimous Declaration
of the Thirteen United States of America

When, in the course of human events, it becomes necessary for one people to dissolve the political bands which have connected them with another, and to assume among the powers of the earth, the separate and equal station to which the laws of Nature and of Nature's God entitle them, a decent respect to the opinions of mankind requires that they should declare the causes which impel them to the separation.

We hold these truths to be self-evident, that all men are created equal, that they are endowed by their Creator with certain unalienable rights, that among these are life, liberty and the pursuit of happiness. That to secure these rights, governments are instituted among men, deriving their just powers from the consent of the governed. That whenever any form of government becomes destructive to these ends, it is the right of the people to alter or to abolish it, and to institute new government, laying its foundation on such principles and organizing its powers in such form, as to them shall seem most likely to effect their safety and happiness. Prudence, indeed, will dictate that governments long established should not be changed for light and transient causes; and accordingly all experience hath shown that mankind are more disposed to suffer, while evils are sufferable, than to right themselves by abolishing the forms to which they are accustomed. But when a long train of abuses and usurpations, pursuing invariably the same object evinces a design to reduce them under absolute despotism, it is their right, it is their duty, to throw off such government, and to provide new guards for their future security. Such has been the patient sufferance of these colonies, and such is now the necessity which constrains them to alter their former systems of government. The history of the present King of Great Britain is a history of repeated injuries and usurpations, all having in direct object the establishment of an absolute tyranny over these states. To prove this, let facts be submitted to a candid world.

He has refused his assent to laws, the most wholesome and necessary for the public good.

He has forbidden his governors to pass laws of immediate and pressing importance, unless suspended in their operation till his assent should be obtained; and when so suspended, he has utterly neglected to attend to them.

He has refused to pass other laws for the accommodation of large districts of people, unless those people would relinquish the right of representation in the legislature, a right inestimable to them and formidable to tyrants only.

He has called together legislative bodies at places unusual, uncomfortable, and distant from the depository of their public records, for the sole purpose of fatiguing them into compliance with his measures.

He has dissolved representative houses repeatedly, for opposing with manly firmness his invasions on the rights of the people.

He has refused for a long time, after such dissolutions, to cause others to be elected; whereby the legislative powers, incapable of annihilation, have returned to the people at large for their exercise; the state remaining in the meantime exposed to all the dangers of invasion from without, and convulsions within.

He has endeavored to prevent the population of these states; for that purpose obstructing the laws for naturalization of foreigners; refusing to pass others to encourage their migration hither, and raising the conditions of new appropriations of lands.

He has obstructed the administration of justice, by refusing his assent to laws for establishing judiciary powers.

He has made judges dependent on his will alone, for the tenure of their offices, and the amount and payment of their salaries.

He has erected a multitude of new offices, and sent hither swarms of officers to harass our people, and eat out their substance.

He has kept among us, in times of peace, standing armies without the consent of our legislature.

He has affected to render the military independent of and superior to civil power.

He has combined with others to subject us to a jurisdiction foreign to our Constitution, and unacknowledged by our laws; giving his assent to their acts of pretended legislation:

For quartering large bodies of armed troops among us:

For protecting them, by mock trial, from punishment for any murders which they should commit on the inhabitants of these states:

For cutting off our trade with all parts of the world:

For imposing taxes on us without our consent:

For depriving us in many cases, of the benefits of trial by jury:

For transporting us beyond seas to be tried for pretended offenses:

For abolishing the free system of English laws in a neighboring province, establishing therein an arbitrary government, and enlarging its boundaries so as to render it at once an example and fit instrument for introducing the same absolute rule in these colonies:

For taking away our charters, abolishing our most valuable laws and altering fundamentally the forms of our governments:

For suspending our own legislatures, and declaring themselves invested with power to legislate for us in all cases whatsoever.

He has abdicated government here, by declaring us out of his protection and waging war against us.

He has plundered our seas, ravaged our coasts, burned our towns, and destroyed the lives of our people.

He is at this time transporting large armies of foreign mercenaries to complete the works of death, desolation and tyranny, already begun with circumstances of cruelty and perfidy scarcely paralleled in the most barbarous ages, and totally unworthy the head of a civilized nation.

He has constrained our fellow citizens taken captive on the high seas to bear arms against their country, to become the executioners of their friends and brethren, or to fall themselves by their hands.

He has excited domestic insurrections amongst us, and has endeavored to bring on the inhabitants of our frontiers, the merciless Indian savages, whose known rule of warfare, is undistinguished destruction of all ages, sexes and conditions.

In every stage of these oppressions we have petitioned for redress in the most humble terms: our repeated petitions have been answered only by repeated injury. A prince, whose character is thus marked by every act which may define a tyrant, is unfit to be the ruler of a free people.

Nor have we been wanting in attention to our British brethren. We have warned them from time to time of attempts by their legislature to extend an unwarrantable jurisdiction over us. We have reminded them of the circumstances of our emigration and settlement here. We have appealed to their native justice and magnanimity, and we have conjured them by the ties of our common kindred to disavow these usurpations, which, would inevitably interrupt our connections and correspondence. They too have been deaf to the voice of justice and of consanguinity. We must, therefore, acquiesce in the necessity, which denounces our separation, and hold them, as we hold the rest of mankind, enemies in war, in peace friends.

We, therefore, the Representatives of the United States of America, in General Congress, Assembled, appealing to the Supreme Judge of the world for the rectitude of our intentions, do, in the name, and by the authority of the good people of these colonies, solemnly publish and declare, that these united colonies are, and of right ought to be free and independent states; that they are absolved from all allegiance to the British Crown, and that all political connection between them and the state of Great Britain, is and ought to be totally dissolved; and that as free and independent states, they have full power to levy war, conclude peace, contract alliances, establish commerce, and to do all other acts and things which independent states may of right do. And for the support of this declaration, with a firm reliance on the protection of Divine Providence, we mutually pledge to each other our lives, our fortunes and our sacred honor.

Signers of the Unanimous Declaration:

New Hampshire

    Josiah Bartlett

    William Whipple

    Matthew Thornton

Massachusetts

    John Hancock

    Samual Adams

    John Adams

    Robert Treat Paine

    Elbridge Gerry

Rhode Island

    Stephen Hopkins

    William Ellery

Connecticut

    Roger Sherman

    Samuel Huntington

    William Williams

    Oliver Wolcott

New York

    William Floyd

    Philip Livingston

    Francis Lewis

    Lewis Morris

New Jersey

    Richard Stockton

    John Witherspoon

    Francis Hopkinson

    John Hart

    Abraham Clark

Pennsylvania

    Robert Morris

    Benjamin Rush

Benjamin Franklin

John Morton

George Clymer

James Smith

George Taylor

James Wilson

George Ross

Delaware

Caesar Rodney

George Read

Thomas McKean

Maryland

Samuel Chase

William Paca

Thomas Stone

Charles Carroll of Carrollton

Virginia

George Wythe

Richard Henry Lee

Thomas Jefferson

Benjamin Harrison

Thomas Nelson, Jr.

Francis Lightfoot Lee

Carter Braxton

North Carolina

William Hooper

Joseph Hewes

John Penn

South Carolina

Edward Rutledge

Thomas Heyward, Jr.

Thomas Lynch, Jr.

Arthur Middleton

Georgia

Button Gwinnett

Lyman Hall

George Walton

Bibliography

QUOTES

Jefferson, Thomas. Writing to John Taylor, 1816. ME 15:23.
"Thomas Jefferson on Politics and Government."
http://etext.lib.virginia.edu/jefferson/quotations/jeff1325.htm

Cooper, Anderson. CNN, "Anderson Cooper 360." April 15, 2009.
http://newsbusters.org/blogs/matthew-balan/2009/04/15/cnns
anderson-cooper-its-hard-talk-when-youre-teabagging#ixzz0m8sxyxEo

Garofalo, Janeane. MSNBC, "Countdown with Keith Olbermann."
April 15, 2009. www.Youtube.com

Reid, Harry. KTNV.com news report. March 27, 2010
www.Youtube.com

Rich, Frank. "Welcome to Confederate History Month." New York Times
Op-Ed. April 17, 2010.
http://www.nytimes.com/2010/04/18/opinion/18rich.htm

Obama, Barack. NBC, "The Today Show." Intv. by Matt Lauer.
Clip at The Washington Post: PostPartisan by Jonathan Capehart.
March 30, 2010.
http://voices.washingtonpost.com/postpartisan/2010/03/president
obama_hears_the_tea.html

Pelosi, Nancy. KTVU Interview. Youtube.com. April 15, 2009.

THE SHERIFF

Hodge, Scott A. "Number of Americans Outside the Income Tax System
Continues to Grow." June 5, 2005.
http://www.taxfoundation.org/research/show/542.html.

Maynor, Jeff. "Ashtabula County: Judge tells residents to "Arm themselves."
WKYC News Story. April 9, 2010.
http://www.wkyc.com/news/local/news_article.aspx?storyid=133951
&catid=3

THE GOLD-STAR MOM

Pelosi, Nancy. "Pelosi Remarks at the 2010 Legislative Conference for National
    Association of Counties." March 9, 2010.
       http://www.speaker.gov/newsroom/pressreleases?id=1576

Lee, Debbie. www.AmericasWoundedWarriors.org

THE RETIREES

"Denmark Tax Rates." http://www.taxrates.cc/html/denmark-tax-rates.html.

Dougherty , Carter. "High income taxes in Denmark worsen a labor shortage."
    The New York Times. December 5, 2007.
       http://www.nytimes.com/2007/12/05/business/worldbusiness/05iht-
       labor.4.8603880.html

THE TEA PARTY ENGINEER

Santelli, Rick. "Rick Santelli's Shout Heard 'Round the World."
    CNBC.com. February 19, 2009.
       http://www.cnbc.com/id/29283701/Rick_Santelli_s_Shout_Heard_
       Round_the_World

THE DECLARATION OF INDEPENDENCE

Transcribed from "the Unanimous Declaration of the Thirteen United States of
    America." July 4, 1776.

About the Author

Steve Ference is an award-winning television news reporter who lives in New York's Capital Region with his wife. Working at various news stations over the last decade, he's covered the deployment of troops to the wars in Afghanistan and Iraq, visits by Presidents Bill Clinton and Barack Obama, and political races at the national and local levels. He has also extensively reported on the economic crisis. Steve covered a number of high-profile trials, including local and federal terrorism cases, and he reported on the Christopher Porco murder trial which received national attention. It became the subject of his first book, "November Memories: Inside the Christopher Porco Case." Steve has also appeared on "Forensic Files."

Steve graduated from Ithaca College with a degree in Politics and Broadcast Journalism. He has worked as a journalist in Washington, DC, as well as in Hartford, Connecticut, and Savannah, Georgia.

You can reach Steve or follow him on twitter.com: SteveFerence1

For my wife, whose love, constant support, editing suggestions, and strength, are far more than a husband could ever ask for.

I would like to thank God for guiding me down another path less traveled, and my family for their love and support.

I thank my father for his advice that surely made the book more palatable to the reader. Thank you.

I would also like to thank Zach, who helped me see there was more to the Tea Parties than I had first thought. Thank you for the most insightful political debates.

And – I would also like to thank each individual in this book who, quite honestly, took a chance by talking with me, hoping that I would fairly explain their perspective. Thank you for the candid discussions, taking time out of your busy lives, and for your willingness to answer my questions and participate in what I believe is a simple, but powerful idea. It will be up to the reader to decide how valuable an endeavor it has been.

Those who have helped me are too numerous to name, but you know who you are, and I am indebted to you.

More from Some of Those Who Were Interviewed for This Book:

Earl Wallace

Website: www.threedimensionalleader.com

Book: The Three-Dimensional Leader

Debbie Lee

Website: www.americasmightywarriors.org

James Ostrowski

Book: Direct Citizen Action: How We Can Win the Second American
        Revolution Without Firing a Shot

Michael Badnarik

Website: www.constitutionpreservation.org

Book: Good to be the King: The Foundation of our Constitutional Freedom

Wade Abbott

Website: www.thisordinarycitizen.wordpress.com

Books Some Interviewees Repeatedly Referenced:

The Creature from Jekyll Island by G. Edward Griffin

End the Fed by Ron Paul

Websites Some Interviewees Repeatedly Referenced:

Campaign for Liberty: www.campaignforliberty.com

Libertarian Financial Political Site: www.LewRockwell.com

Oathkeepers Organization: www.oathkeepers.org

We The People Foundation: www.wethepeoplefoundation.org

(These books and web sites are offered as a place to read more about some of the issues discussed in this book. They were recommended by those who were interviewed, and are not endorsed or un-endorsed by the author, and may not be related to the topic of Tea Parties.)

ALSO BY STEVE FERENCE:

NOVEMBER MEMORIES: Inside the Christopher Porco Case

A

True Crime Novel

In the middle of the night, a father is murdered and a mother is left for dead after a brutal ax attack. Before doctors try to save the woman's life, police say she told them her son is the one who did it – even though he's attending a prestigious college over three hours away. As the boy's mother hangs on for dear life, she wakes up in the hospital with no memory of the attack, and believes her son to be innocent of the crime. But investigators are sure they've got their man - Christopher Porco – a tall, handsome student with plenty of debt and bad grades. It's a murder that shattered a family, shook the New York Capital Region, and made national news. The book takes you from the murder scene to the verdict, providing an unprecedented look at the evidence and allegations – from DNA to possible Mafia involvement – in a case that's as unbelievable as it is true.